HISPANIC HERITAGE: VOLUME 1

ANCIENT EMPIRES & MIGHTY PEOPLE

RICHARD SANCHEZ

Published by Abdo & Daughters, 4940 Viking Drive, Suite 622, Edina, MN 55435.

Library bound edition distributed by Rockbottom Books, Pentagon Tower, P.O. Box 36036, Minneapolis, Minnesota 55435.

Photos by:
Bettmann Archive: 5, 7, 25, 27
Archive Photos: 13, 14, 19, 21, 23, 26, 29, 40

Edited by John Hamilton

Library of Congress Cataloging–in–Publication Data
Sanchez, Richard, 1954-
    Ancient empires & might people / Richard Sanchez
        p.   cm — (Hispanic heritage)
    Includes bibliographical references (p.) and index.
    ISBN 1-56239-331-6
    1. Indians—Antiquities—Juvenile literature. 2. America—Antiquities—Juvenile literature. I. Title. II. Title: Ancient empires and mighty people. III. Series: Hispanic heritage (Edina. Minn.)
E61.S257   1994
970.01—dc20   94-15860
                                    CIP
                                    AC

CONTENTS

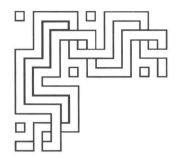

1
INTRODUCTION

The United States is called the land of the free and home of the brave. It is these things because Hispanics have helped make it that way. Since the beginning of this nation and long before, Hispanics played important roles in bringing about hope, liberty and justice for all.

This is the story of some of the ancestors of today's Hispanics in the United States.

Our trip back through time takes us first to the Stone Age. This is where United States history for Hispanic people really begins.

The pyramids of Teotihuacan in Mexico, about 40 miles from Mexico City. Teotihuacan was North America's first planned city, with a grid system aligned with the city's center. The pyramids, including the Pyramid of the Moon, shown here, rival the pyramids of Egypt in size and complexity. Little today is know of the builders of this ancient city, but the pyramids were probably built to honor their gods.

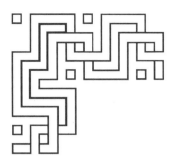

2
AN EMPTY PLACE

The United States is on the continent of North America. In the Stone Age, there was no one here. Only animals and birds and fish and insects.

The first people to arrive were among the ancestors of today's Hispanics. They came from Asia. They got here by walking. Scientists who study the past say these earliest settlers crossed over from Asia up near the North Pole. There, Asia and North America are only about 50 miles apart. Somehow the narrow stretch of ocean between the two continents at that point must have frozen over so people could walk across the water. Or, maybe, there was a strip of land connecting the two and it later sank into the ocean.

Once they arrived in North America, these people headed south. They kept walking and walking. About three miles a week. Until, finally, they reached what eventually would become the United States.

Some of the ancestors of the Hispanics settled in the southwestern part of the future United States. Others continued south into Central America and toward the Caribbean Sea. Still others went farther and didn't stop until they came to the southern tip of South America.

Meanwhile, a group of people from the warm south of Asia went by boat across the China Sea to settle what one day would be known as the Philippine Islands. From here, too, would come ancestors of today's Hispanic-Americans.

They Brought Skills

Wherever they went, many of those who migrated from Asia brought with them the skills needed to survive and prosper in the new worlds they pioneered.

They produced baskets to carry wild grains and fruits from the fields back to their camps. Later, as they began to farm the land, the baskets were used to collect the harvest of crops. They made snares and nets to trap wild animals.

They also made weapons. Two of the most common were spears and arrows.

The clothes worn by the people were not made of animal skins but of cloth. They had learned to take plants and pull from them fibers that could be woven together to make fabric.

The Discovery of Corn

The single most important event for these settlers in the Americas was the discovery of corn, or maize.

It is thought the discovery may have taken place in Central America. What was so important about it was that the people no longer had to wander in search of wild-growing food. They could stay in one place and build real homes, villages, cities, even empires. Corn freed the people to develop great and mighty civilizations.

Maize (another word for corn) was probably first used as food in Central America.

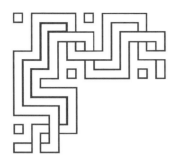

3

SETTLERS OF THE SOUTHWEST

The people who settled in North America's southwest region found it hot, dry and barren. The homes they built were carved out of cliffs. Some chose to live in huts made of clay and timbers. Either way, the insides of the homes stayed cool in the summer and warm in the winter because mud and rock make good insulation. Communities of these homes are known today as pueblos.

One of the most famous pueblos is Oraibi in Arizona, founded by the Hopi people about 1,000 years ago. Another interesting one is Acoma in New Mexico. Acoma is built atop a mesa 350 feet high. The builders had to drag the heavy wood timbers with their bare hands from a forest 20 miles away. Not far away from Acoma is Enchanted Mesa. The people had to abandon Enchanted Mesa after a powerful earthquake destroyed the narrow walkway leading to their homes up the steep cliff while they were all down in the valley working their farms.

Pueblos were built into cliffs and on top of mesas to protect the people against enemy attack. The heights made it easy for the defenders to bomb their attackers by raining down on them load after load of heavy rocks. The heights further worked

Cliff dwellings were easy to defend from enemy attack. Invaders could be bombed from above with heavy rocks.

against the attackers because the force of gravity made spears and arrows thrown up toward the pueblo sputter out before reaching their targets.

ARTS & CRAFTS

The people of the North American southwest grew famous for their arts and crafts. They were expert silversmiths. They also created many beautiful pieces of jewelry from stones such as turquoise. And they used clay to make wonderful pottery.

Dance was an important part of pueblo life. Dance was performed to give delight to various gods worshipped by the people. Each dance was part prayer and part story. Dancers usually wore costumes to portray the gods.

FARMING

Although the climate was usually dry, the people were able to grow corn and beans by building irrigation ditches. The ditches allowed water from rivers and ponds to flow into the fields. Sometimes the nearest water source was many miles away so the ditches had to be very long.

Everyone in the pueblos had a job to do. Men and boys hunted, dug for precious stones or kept the water flowing through the irrigation ditches. Women and girls spun cloth, made pottery and ground the corn into meal for baking a kind of tortilla.

In the early 13th Century, there was a long, terrible time of no rain. The rivers and ponds dried up. The corn did not grow. As a result, many pueblo citizens died of starvation and thirst. Those who were left alive moved away in search of food. Many of the pueblos around this time were turned into ghost towns. Meanwhile, enough of them still had water and food to survive. When the rains finally came, life was restored and new pueblos were built.

RANGE OF THE MAYA, AZTEC AND INCA CIVILIZATIONS

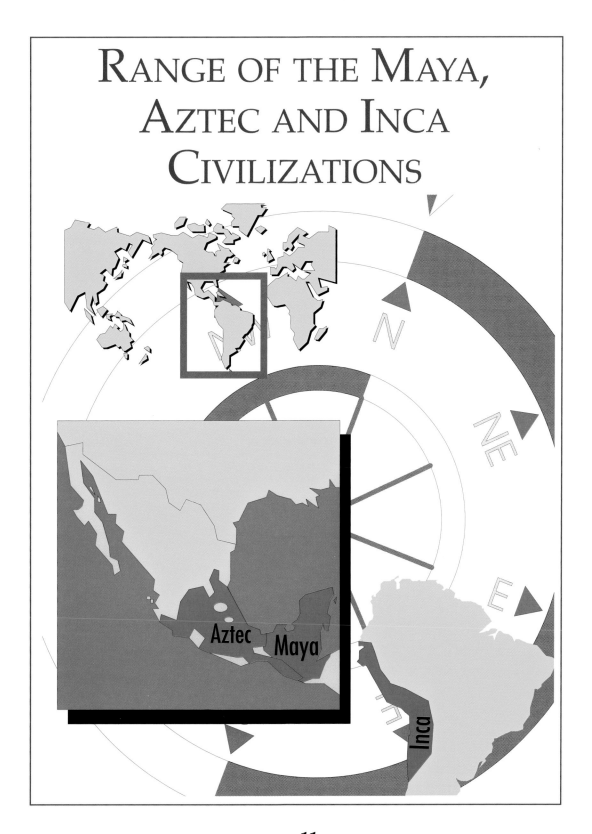

4
THE MAYA

There have been many intelligent groups of people throughout history. Yet, scientists say there have been few who could match the genius of a group known as the Maya. They were the discoverers of corn. They even invented a calendar to tell them exactly the day to plant the corn so they could grow more of it than anyone else.

In the days of the Maya, corn was prized even more than gold. And the Maya had plenty of both. In fact, they had so much corn and gold that they gave them to neighboring tribes and nations in exchange for other products. The Maya became very wealthy by doing this.

UNITED THEY STOOD

The Maya began rising as a mighty nation around 3000 B.C. in what now is Guatemala, Honduras and southern Mexico. At first, the Maya were not ruled by a single leader. They were many tribes that joined forces. What held them together was they all spoke the same language, shared the same beliefs and had the same interests. They realized it was better to put aside their differences and focus on things they had in common. The Maya also knew that if they did not unite they would end up fighting with one another and never become great.

The Mayan culture developed steadily over the

next several thousands of years. During this period, fantastic temples were built. Many of them stand even to this day. The temples are so beautiful and amazingly built that they are considered wonders of the New World.

DECLINE, REBIRTH & MORE DECLINE

Mayan architecture was at its most creative from 472 A.D. to 620 A.D. After that time, the Maya entered a period of decline. No new temples were built. The people became unhappy and quarreled among themselves. As a nation, they grew weak.

Finally, invaders from the area that now is northern Mexico attacked and captured many Mayan

The pyramid that invading Conquistadors called Castillo (Castle) sits at Chichen Itza in Mexico's Yucatan Peninsula. Chichen Itza was one of the most important Mayan cities.

Chichen Itza's El Castillo pyramid
is a large temple on a mound about
one acre in area and rising to a
height of 100 feet, with staircases
leading up on four sides to the
temple of Kukulcan at the top.

Mayan pottery was often decorated
with images of gods and scenes of
battle.

cities. These invaders were the Toltec. Gradually, Toltec ways combined with Maya ways and a new Mayan kingdom was born from the ashes of the old.

By the 10th Century, there again was progress in the land. Especially on the Yucatan Peninsula. It was an era of much prosperity for the Maya. They even started colonies in the Gulf Coast region of the future United States.

Sadly, this time of new greatness did not last forever. Two hundred years later, the new Mayan tribes were again in trouble. Civil war broke out. The battles went on and on. By the 1500s, the Maya were getting close to destroying themselves.

What was the fighting all about? Some believe it started when the chiefs of two major cities got into a jealous battle over a beautiful woman each wanted to marry. Much more likely, the problem was a serious shortage of corn.

The land in which the Maya lived was largely covered by thick jungles. To grow corn, room for farming had to be made. This meant cutting down parts of the jungle. The Maya had to work very hard to keep the jungle from growing back. However, something must have happened to prevent the farmers from clearing enough land to grow as much food as was needed. Maybe volcanos erupted and ruined the land by covering it with lava and ash. Maybe heavy rains washed away nutrients from the soil no longer protected by its jungle covering and the corn could not grow properly as a result. Or maybe the rulers were demanding too much taxes and so the people rebelled by not working. It's a mystery.

SCIENTIFIC EXCELLENCE

The Maya left behind an incredible legacy in the field of science. The calendar they invented divided the year into 18 months of 20 days each, with four extra days at the end of the final month. That added up to 364 days, almost identical to the number of days in our modern calendar. It is so accurate that an error occurs in it once only every 30,000 years.

How did the Maya figure out something like that? By carefully keeping track of the movements of the sun, moon, planets and stars across the sky. They did this for centuries and wrote down everything they learned. When they had collected enough information, they were ready to invent the calendar.

Writing down the things they observed in the heavens required an alphabet and a number system. These the Maya had to invent as well. Their alphabet was not at all like ours. They used pictures to represent spoken sounds and ideas. We do not know how to read Mayan writings because the secret of what the pictures mean was lost when the last Mayan religious leader died in 1626. Only the leaders knew how to read and write.

Their number system used a series of dots and dashes to represent numerals. One dot meant 1, one dash meant 5. It was like Roman numerals. But one thing the Mayan numerals had that others lacked was zero. It took the clever Mayans to figure out the concept of zero in mathematics. This was one of their greatest contributions to science as we know and use it today.

IMPORTANCE OF THE TEMPLES

Temples built by the Maya were shaped like the pyramids of Egypt. The difference was the Mayan pyramids were cut off at the top. This cut-off formed a flat deck. On it, the Maya built altars and shrines.

Spectacular ceremonies were held at these temples. Priests marched up along the stairs that ringed the temples all the way to their tops. The priests often led the ceremonies while wearing feathered masks. Sweet-smelling incense and clouds of colorful smoke would fill the air. Thousands of citizens lined the streets at the base of these temples to watch in awe and wonder.

The most important religious leaders were known as high priests. Although they had the power to order almost anyone to do almost anything at any time, these high priests were rarely seen in public. They only came out for big ceremonies. By staying out of sight until then, it caused people to think of the high priests as gods themselves.

The high priests were worshipped, and this helped them gain more control over the tribal chiefs. The high priests also were the keepers of knowledge about such things as when the next eclipse of the sun was going to occur. Ordinary people weren't allowed to know that eclipses could be predicted by using mathematics. This way, the high priests could trick the people into believing they had the power to make the sun go dark. Not knowing any better, the people were terrified into obeying the high priests rather than have the sun taken away as punishment.

Looking Into Space

Religion was only part of the purpose of the temples. They also served as observatories. An observatory is a place where scientists gather to study the movements of the planets and the stars.

Some temples were designed to be giant sundials. Sundials are devices used for telling time during daylight hours. Other temples were built in such a way that the Maya could tell planting season had arrived just by being able to view a certain planet or star from a tiny window inside the observatory.

Building such temples required tremendous skill. And they erected them without the help of oxen or metal tools. Construction began by piling huge amounts of earth into the rough shape of a pyramid. Next, the builders laid giant stone blocks into place. The stones were cemented together. Usually, the blocks had art carved into them. Sometimes, the blocks were covered with stucco and painted.

The architects of these temples used the same designs and building methods century after century. When a temple outlived its usefulness, the Maya simply covered it with earth and built a new one on top of the old. Temples were often grouped together with palaces around a plaza. The plazas were the place where the people gathered to watch ceremonies and big events.

Waging War

Like nearly all nations throughout history, the Maya relied on an army of warriors to protect themselves from attack. Mayan soldiers wore hel-

Chichen Itza's Caracol building was used by the Maya as an observatory to study the movements of the planets and the stars.

mets and padded armor. They used spears and arrows as their main weapons of combat.

The warriors often tried to capture rather than kill their enemies. Captured enemies could be useful as palace slaves or as human sacrifices to the gods. Toward the end of the Mayan civilization, the rulers were forced to hire armies made up of ferocious Aztec warriors from Northern Mexico because too many Mayan soldiers had lost their will to fight.

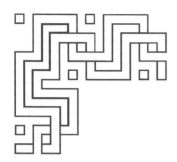

6
THE AZTEC

The Aztecs came from a territory then called Aztlan. Aztlan stretched from the most northern part of modern Mexico to parts of California, Arizona, New Mexico and Texas. Scientists say this explains why the language of the Aztec was so similar to that spoken by the natives of southwest North America.

As the Aztec migrated southward into Mexico, they followed a route along the coast. They finally settled along the shore of Lake Texcoco. At that time, another civilization called the Toltec were still strong enough to defend themselves against the Aztec. A peace treaty was signed by the Toltec and the Aztec. The Toltec agreed to let the Aztec live near the lake. But the land they were given was just a swamp. It was worthless for farming or building houses.

Fortunately, the Aztec were not quitters. They got right to work and made rafts from the reeds and twigs they found. Then, they launched the rafts onto the lake and tied them together to create a huge floating platform. Long poles were driven

At right, examples of Aztec costumes and arms.

into the bottom of the lake and the platform was anchored to them. Next, the engineers hauled mud up from the bottom and spread it across the platform. They kept adding more mud until at last the Aztec had turned the platform into a man-made island.

More platforms were built and the island-making process was repeated. Then, they planted gardens and raised all the food they needed. Huts were built so the people could live in comfort and safety on the islands. From these islands would later arise a city. The Aztec called this place Tenochtitlan. It became their capital. And what a beautiful city it was!

Meanwhile, the Toltec grew weaker as a nation while the Aztec grew stronger. In 1380, the Aztec forced the Toltec to give them the right to draw delicious fresh water from the springs of Chapultepec. About 50 years later, the Aztec Emperor Itzcouatl crushed an important army of the Toltec. He forced the remaining Toltec soldiers to switch to his side. With their help, Itzcouatl was able to take control of the land all the way down to the border of what today is Guatemala.

FORERUNNER OF MODERN DEMOCRACY

The first Aztec emperors were elected to office from among the leading citizens by a body of tribal chiefs. But as the decades rolled by and the emperors added to their power, it became common for emperors upon their death to pass the throne to a brother or cousin.

The emperor was in charge of tribal chiefs. Each tribe lived in its own district and selected as its chief

the most wise, brave and wealthy warrior of all. Once selected, the chief shared his power with a leader called The Snake Woman. The chief took care of military matters while The Snake Woman looked after the needs of the workers. Both the chief and The Snake Woman received advice from a council made up of the most important citizens.

The Sun Stone was used as a kind of calendar by the Aztecs. In the center of the 20-ton carving is the Aztec Sun God.

THE LAST EMPEROR

The last emperor of the Aztec civilization was Montezuma. His palace was in Tenochtitlan. His power over the people was awesome. None of the ordinary citizens dared look at him for fear he would have them killed. Even the rulers who served him were afraid to look him in the eye. Montezuma believed himself too good even to let his feet be dirtied by contact with the ground. For that reason he was carried everywhere by servants. When he did choose to walk, his servants placed cloth along his path. Montezuma was famous for the colorful gold headdress and jeweled sandals he wore.

Human sacrifice occurred regularly during Aztec religious ceremonies. The humans sacrificed were usually captured enemy soldiers. But Aztec slaves and even children were sometimes used as sacrifices. The sacrifices were made to please the gods of the Aztec. The need for sacrifices was so great that the Aztec tried to remain constantly at war so that there would be a steady supply of captives. In 1487, the Aztec sacrificed 20,000 people to celebrate the opening of a grand new temple.

AZTEC LAW

Honesty and obeying the law were very important to the Aztec. They set up a system of courts so people could settle their arguments peacefully. There were four branches of the court. All four branches were located in Tenochtitlan. Each branch heard only a certain type of case and the verdicts were made by a judge and two assistants. Three bailiffs were assigned to each branch. Their job was to make sure the verdicts were immediately carried out.

One of the main laws of the Aztec was that the land belonged to all the people. However, citizens first had to get a lease from the rulers in order to farm the land. Each person's lease was good for two years. At the end of the two years, the farmer had to prove he or she used the land wisely and was productive. Then the farmer was given another two-year lease. The lease was taken away and given to someone else if a farmer was found to be using the land unwisely or was unproductive.

Aztecs who worked hard enough could become wealthy. The richer ones owned slaves. However, slaves enjoyed some freedoms. For example, they could own a home and they could work for themselves after completing their slave duties for the day. Slaves even could have slaves of their own.

Education played a role in Aztec life. But learning was only for the children of leaders and the wealthy. Beginning at age 6, these children were taught to read, write and solve math problems. They also studied history, religion and art.

Above: *An Aztec funeral vase.*
Right: *A stone sculpture of the Aztec rain god, Tlaloc.*

7
THE INCA

Another mighty empire of the Americas was that of the Inca. The Inca lived in the Andes Mountains of South America. Their empire started in the Cuzco Valley of Peru. It began around the 13th Century. There isn't much known about the ancestors of the Inca before that time.

More is known about the various peoples conquered by the Inca. The Cuzco Valley was settled nearly 3,000 years before the Inca arrived. Villages became towns. Then some of the towns became cities. The natives built temples similar to those of the Maya. There even was an empire that arose called the Huari. The Huari empire later collapsed and vanished. That happened around the year 1000 A.D. The departure of the Huari paved the way for the Inca to get started.

Once the Inca Empire formed, it took only 200 years for them to conquer nations up and down the west coast of South America. At the peak of their power, the Inca empire stretched 2,100 miles from the northern border of Ecuador to near Santiago in Chile. Under Inca control were at least 6 million people of captured lands.

Machu Picchu, the Lost City of the Incas. Discovered by Hiram Bingham in 1911, Machu Picchu sits in the Urumbamba Valley of southern Peru, a very inaccessible part of the Andes Mountains. Some scientists believe many Inca fled here when the Spanish invaded in the 1530's. The Spanish never found Machu Picchu, but after the death of the last Inca emperor, citizens abandoned the city. It remained uninhabited for over 300 years until Bingham's discovery while on an expedition for the National Geographic Society.

LAND OF THE FOUR QUARTERS

The Inca called their territory Tahuantinsuyu. It means Land of the Four Quarters. They called it this because they had divided the country into four districts to make it easier to govern all those conquered people.

The Inca were ruled by a total of 12 emperors. The first was named Manco Capac. He convinced the people that his father was the sun. His palace was filled with luxury furniture and gold decorations. Each new emperor after him built a palace in Cuzco to celebrate the beginning of his reign.

The next seven emperors to follow Manco Capac made the Inca form of government stronger and stronger.

Pachacuti Inca Yupanqui was the ninth emperor. Under his rule, the Inca empire began its march up and down South America. He won battle after battle. So unbeatable were the Inca that many neighboring nations hurried to become friends with Pachacuti rather than risk war. Pachacuti proved himself to be as wise a leader as he was a crafty soldier.

Conquered nations became the property of the Inca. Inca language, religion and law was imposed on the people. However, the Inca allowed those they defeated to keep their own culture and traditions. Their leaders were allowed to stay in power, but their sons were taken as prisoners back to Cuzco as a way of making sure the leaders would do what the Inca wanted.

Inca rule was very strict. The emperor gave all the orders, but before making decisions he would talk to the members of his council. There were four council members. Each member was the ruler of one of the four quarters. These council members usually came from the emperor's own family. They spent most of their time in Cuzco. The job of actually running the quarters was performed by governors whom the council members picked to represent them.

A WEALTH OF TREASURES

Of all the nations and peoples in the Western Hemisphere, the Inca may have owned the most gold and priceless gems. They dug mines in many places in search of precious metals including silver, copper, bronze and tin. Metalworkers used their skill to produce fine tools, weapons and decorations. They traded much of what they made to get more wealth and other things they needed. They were very successful traders who knew how to drive a hard bargain.

The Incas built many beautiful cities. To enter a city, visitors first had to pay a toll and give a good reason for wanting to be there. There was hardly ever any crime because the Inca soldiers who patrolled the streets were quick to punish anyone who broke the law.

This was a people who believed in hard work. Inca citizens liked to help one another build houses. Houses were built of whatever materials were handy—wood, stone, mud or grass.

Excellent roads and bridges were built by Inca engineers to connect their cities and make it easier for news to be carried from one end of the empire to the other. Many of the roads were straight as arrows to shorten travel. Messengers on foot could bring news from any part of the empire to the capital at Cuzco in as little as six days. Such speed was possible in part because the government placed messengers at posts every few miles. The first messenger would run as fast as he could to the post where a second messenger was waiting to receive the information. Then, this second messenger would run as fast as he could to the next post where a third messenger was waiting. On and on it went like that until the final messenger reached Cuzco. The roads were kept clear of traffic so as not to slow down the messengers. Only government officials and messengers were allowed on the roads.

SIGNS OF INVENTIVENESS

The climate along the coast of the Inca empire was dry. Water had to be brought in for crops to grow. The Inca did this by building irrigation canals many miles long. The canals carried water from sources wherever they could be found.

Further inland, up in the mountains, there was plenty of rain for farming. But there was not enough flat land. The Inca solved this problem by carving terraces into the mountainsides. Terraces are planting areas shaped like stair steps. Many kinds of crops can be grown on terraces. The trick is keeping rain and wind from knocking down the terraces. The clever Inca figured out ways to prevent that from happening.

Inca weavers and embroiderers were among the best ever. They made clothes and tapestries that had very complicated designs and patterns in over 200 different colors. The type of clothes and head-dresses worn by a person showed whether he or she was a leader, a craftsman or a laborer. The clothes also showed from where in the empire that person had come. In the cool mountains, people wore heavy wool clothes made from the hair of llamas. Down along the warm coastal deserts, people wore clothes made of light cotton.

OTHER ACHIEVEMENTS

The Inca loved to study the moon, the planets and the stars. They became excellent astronomers. The records they kept about the heavenly bodies were very detailed and very accurate.

And the Incas knew much about medicine. They developed the art and science of surgery.

The Inca also greatly enjoyed music. Flutes and drums were favorite instruments. And, wherever there is music, dancing is sure to follow. That was certainly true of the Inca. Nearly all their religious ceremonies and public festivals combined music and dance. When the Inca danced, they acted out stories about life in their world.

8
SETTLERS OF THE ISLANDS

To the east of Central America lies the Caribbean Sea. There are a number of islands in it that were settled by people whose ancestors came originally from Asia. These include Puerto Rico and Cuba.

Settlers probably reached these islands by walking there. Scientists say many thousands of years ago there may have been a land bridge connecting the islands to South America, just as there was an ice bridge between Asia and North America. The land bridge vanished several thousands of years ago. It may have sunk into the sea.

Coming as they may have from South America, these island dwellers brought with them the skills necessary to make tools and raise crops. On Puerto Rico, the people were blessed with especially rich soil that made it easy to grow many delicious foods.

The settlers in Puerto Rico, Cuba and the other Caribbean islands generally lived quiet, peaceful lives. In the Lesser Antilles islands there was one group of people known as the Carib. They were bloodthirsty. The Carib frequently attacked other people and took them prisoner. They would bring the captives back to their cities, kill them and use their bodies for food.

THE PHILIPPINES

On the other side of the world, off the southern coast of Asia, is a group of islands known today as the Philippines. In prehistoric times, colonists from Asia settled in the Philippines. The earliest people to arrive there built crude shelters from tree branches and leaves. They were hunters and gatherers who ate mostly roots, snakes, and lizards.

Next to arrive in the Philippines were migrants from the southeast part of Asia. They drove out most of the original settlers from the plains and valleys and forced them into the hills. These newcomers could fight. They made trophies of the heads of enemies they had beaten.

The newcomers were extremely inventive and industrious. As they began to move into the hills, they built terraces just like the Inca of South America to grow crops. But instead of corn, the main crop of these people was rice. Rice requires lots and lots of water to grow. They grew rice on the mountain terraces. That was an amazing feat because the weight of all that water in the soil should have made the terraces collapse and tumble down the sides of the mountains. But the terraces stayed put. Even today, this feat is considered one of the world's greatest engineering achievements.

Later, a third group of settlers arrived. They migrated from a different part of southeast Asia. They were called Filipino. Although they were wise and brave, the second group of settlers was no match for the Filipino. Eventually, the Filipino took over nearly all of the Philippine Islands and became its leading culture for centuries to come.

In the 13th Century, one group of Filipinos became famous as soldiers and pirates. They sailed in boats across the China Sea and launched raids on mainland Asia.

Other Filipino were skilled metalworkers. They also knew how to dive for pearls in the warm waters surrounding the islands. They fished and farmed. They did not become fabulously wealthy like the Maya, Aztec and Inca nations. However, they had riches enough to satisfy their needs.

9
EPILOGUE

The peoples you have just read about were the early settlers of lands that later would give rise to the Hispanic world. First they were explorers, then they became conquerors. They also were strong in their religious beliefs and they wanted the people of the lands they conquered to share those same beliefs.

Beginning in the late 1490s, there came from Europe men who would continue this pattern of exploration, conquest and religious conversion. These were the seafaring men of Spain and Portugal. They would forever change the lives of the first settlers.

GLOSSARY

ARCHITECTURE

Designing a building or using certain types of construction materials so that it looks a certain way when completed.

BAILIFF

The person in charge of prisoners who have been brought into court for a trial.

CIVILIZATION

The highly developed art, science, religion and government of a group of people.

COLONY

A place where people from another nation go to live and work as group. They do not govern themselves but are under the control of the nation they left behind.

CONTINENT

A great mass of land. There are seven such land masses covering the face of the earth.

COUNCIL

A group of people brought together to make laws or solve problems.

CULTURE

The arts, history, and activities of a group of people.

EMPEROR

The leader of many nations or lands.

INCENSE
A powder that gives off a sweet smell when burned.

IRRIGATION
To deliver water to a farm field through one or more ditches, channels or streams.

LEASE
An agreement by the owner of a property to let another person use it for a certain amount of time in exchange for payment.

NUTRIENTS
Minerals in the ground that make farm crops grow big and healthy.

PYRAMID
A building with a square or rectangle base and four triangle sides that meet at the top.

SACRIFICES
A ceremony in which a person or an animal is killed as a gift to one or more gods.

TEMPLE
A building where people go to worship their god or gods.

TERRACE
Ground on the side of a hill that has been made flat for farming by shaping the soil up and down the slope into the form of stair steps.

TRIBE
A group of people who share the same customs, language and history.

BIBLIOGRAPHY

Baity, Elizabeth Chesley. *Americans Before Columbus*. Viking Press. New York. 1961

Kendall, Sarita. *The Incas*. New Discovery Books, New York. 1992.

Lepthien, Emilie U. *The Philippines*. Childrens Press, Chicago. 1984.

Memmi, Albert. *Colonizer and the Colonized*. Orion Press, New York. 1965.

Stuart, Gene S. and George E. *Lost Kingdoms of the Maya*. National Geographic Society, Washington D.C. 1993.

Tuck, Jay N. and Vergara, Norma C. *Heroes of Puerto Rico*. Fleet Press, New York. 1969.

Various contributors. *World Book Encyclopedia*. Field Enterprises, Chicago.

Various contributors. *Encyclopaedia Brittanica*. Encyclopaedia Brittanica Inc., London and Chicago.

INDEX

The ruins of Machu Picchu, the Lost City of the Incas, lie silent amid the forbidding peaks of the Andes Mountains.

MAKING CONNECTIONS 2:

An Integrated Approach to Learning English

▲▲▲

MAKING CONNECTIONS 2:

An Integrated Approach to Learning English

Carolyn Kessler

Linda Lee

Mary Lou McCloskey

Mary Ellen Quinn

Lydia Stack

Heinle & Heinle Publishers
An International Thomson Publishing Company
Boston, MA 02116, U.S.A.

I(T)P

▲▲▲

The publication of *Making Connections* was directed by the members of the Heinle & Heinle Secondary ESL Publishing Team:

Editorial Director: Roseanne Mendoza
Senior Production
Services Coordinator: Lisa McLaughlin
Market Development
Director: Ingrid Greenberg
Developmental Editor: Nancy Jordan

Also Participating in the publication of this program were:

Publisher: Stan Galek
Director of Production: Elizabeth Holthaus
Senior Assistant Editor: Sally Conover
Manufacturing Coordinator: Mary Beth Hennebury
Composition: GTS Graphics
Project Management: GTS Graphics
Interior Design: Martucci Studio
Illustration: Jerry Malone/Martucci Studio
Cover Design: Martucci Studio

Manufactured in the United States of America

ISBN: 0-8384-7012-2

Heinle & Heinle Publishers is an International Thomson Publishing Company

10 9 8 7 6 5 4

PREFACE

Middle and High School ESOL (English for Speakers of Other Languages) students are faced with a formidable task. In the few short years of school that remain, they must learn both English and the challenging content of their academic curriculum, made more challenging because so much language acquisition is demanded. *Making Connections: An Integrated Approach to Learning English* provides resources to integrate the teaching and learning of language and academic content. These resources help teachers and students develop students' ability to communicate in English as they focus on motivating themes with topics, activities, tools, and procedures that introduce the content areas of science, social studies, and literature.

Making Connections: An Integrated Approach to Learning English is designed to help secondary students and their teachers reach toward important, essential goals and to facilitate their learning language and content in the ways they learn best. What are the goals we reach for?

Joy—the joy in life and learning that will make our students happy, successful lifetime learners

Literacy—the ability to use reading and writing to accomplish amazing things

Community—the knowledge that they live in an accepting community where they have rights, responsibilities, and resources

Access—access to whatever resources they need to accomplish their own goals, including access to technology

Power—the power to make their lives into whatever they choose

What are the ways of teaching and learning that work best, according to our understanding of language acquisition research? The answer, we believe, is through **integrated learning**. *Making Connections* includes four different kinds of integration: language areas, language and academic content, students with one another, and school with the larger community.

- We integrate language areas through active learning.

We combine reading, writing, listening, and speaking into things that students **do**. Through interaction with authentic and culturally relevant literature, through activities that involve genuine communication, and through student-owned process writing, students learn the "parts" or "skills" of language in meaningful "whole" contexts.

■ We integrate language with academic content and processes.

Language is best learned when it is used as a tool, when students are meaningfully engaged in something important to them. Learning the language and participating in processes specific to the academic content area subjects are essential for preparing students to move into mainstream content-area classrooms. By teaching language through content, we attempt to do several things at once: we help students to learn to use a variety of learning strategies; introduce them to science, social studies and literature content appropriate for their age and grade levels; and help them to use accessible language and learn new essential language in the process.

■ We integrate students with one another.

We help teachers and students develop a real learning community in which students and teacher use a variety of strategies—including many cooperative learning strategies—to accomplish student-owned educational goals. We acknowledge that students are not all at the same level linguistically or academically but recognize that each student has strengths to offer in your classroom, so we provide choices of materials and activities that accommodate a multi-level class.

■ We integrate school with home culture and with the greater community.

We strive for materials and activities that are relevant for a culturally diverse group and that help students to develop their self-esteem by valuing their unique cultural heritages. We seek to involve students in the community and the community with schools by providing and encouraging activities and projects that relate to community life and that put students into interaction with community representatives. This active involvement is integral to the development of students' content-area knowledge and language.

In order to reach toward these goals and implement these four kinds of integration, we have used integrated thematic units as the organizational basis for *Making Connections*. Our themes are arrived at in a variety of ways: some, like "Choosing Foods," have very concrete connections among the sections of the units. Others, like "Waves," make more metaphorical connections among sections that treat very different aspects of the theme. In all the units, students will make connections across content areas and will revisit themes and use and re-use the language of themes in different ways. Each unit provides multi-level information and experiences that integrate language with one or more content areas and includes the following features:

Learning strategies. In each unit, we incorporate strategies to help students with their language and content area learning. We encourage teachers and students to be aware of the applicability of these strategies in new learning situations. Our goal is to create active, capable, self-starting learners.

Cooperative learning. Cooperative learning has been shown to be effective in facilitating both student learning and successful cross-cultural, multi-level student integration. Each unit uses a variety of cooperative groupings and activities to achieve these goals.

Language Focus. Language is learned best in a meaningful, useful context. In *Making Connections*, students use language to accomplish real tasks, many of which they have chosen themselves from activity menus. From these meaningful contexts, many opportunities arise to teach language concepts as they are needed. Both the student text and the teacher's edition contain suggestions for taking advantage of opportunities for teaching language features as these opportunities arise.

Content-area experiences in science, social studies, and literature. We have chosen three content areas for focus in *Making Connections* because of their importance to student success and because of the importance of language to success in these areas. In science, we introduce the language of science (and frequently mathematics language as well) through offering authentic scientific experiences using materials that are accessible to an ESOL teacher. In social studies, we take advantage of the multicultural nature of ESOL classes to introduce the processes of the social sciences. We have provided literature in a variety of genres to enhance content-area learning. As students begin to learn the language, they need to talk about and create their own literary works.

Choices for teachers and students in multicultural, multilevel classrooms. Every ESOL class is a multilevel, multicultural class. In order to meet the needs of these diverse groups and in order to empower both teachers and students, *Making Connections* offers many choices. Teachers can choose among the many activities in the units to provide experiences most appropriate to their classes and can sequence these activities as needed. They can also individualize by choosing different activities for different students within the class. Each unit includes an activity menu of experiences and projects that will help students to integrate and apply the material from the unit. Both teacher and students can make choices among these culminating events to suit them to student interests, level of ability, and needs. Related literary selections following each unit offer additional choices for teachers and students interested in reading extensions.

Since we are teachers as well as authors, we know that the most important aspect of your instructional program is what happens between teacher and student. We have tried to develop a program that offers teachers and students many choices of activities, resources, and ideas that provide chances to interact, learn, and grow. We hope *Making Connections* helps students learn what they need to experience success in school as well as in life. We welcome teacher feedback and students' responses to *Making Connections*.

The authors

Contents

Unit 1 - Choosing Foods

Topics

Unit 2 - Sending Messages

Topics

Unit 3 - Setting Goals

Topics

Unit 4 - Making Changes

Topics

Unit 5 - Resolving Conflict

Topics

MAKING CONNECTIONS *Book 2*

LANGUAGE FOCUS	STUDY STRATEGIES	LITERATURE

Expressing Likes and Dislikes
Asking and Answering Questions
  about Likes and Dislikes
Comparing Likes
Making Polite Requests
Making and Responding to
  Suggestions
Asking and Answering Questions
Giving Measurements
Comparing Two Things
Comparing Three or More Things
	Making a Venn Diagram
	Selective Listening
	Classifying
	Taking Notes in a Chart
	Making Bar Graphs
		How to Eat a Hot
		  Fudge Sundae
		  by Jonathan Holden
		How to Eat a Poem
		  by Eve Merriam
		Watermelons
		  by Charles Simic
		A Round
		  by Eve Merriam

Asking What Something Means
Asking for Information
Reporting What Someone Said
Describing Cause and Effect
Asking for and Giving Information
Making Guesses
Stating an Opinion
Giving Reasons
	Brainstorming
	Using Pictures
	Making a Know/Want to Know
	  Chart
	Classifying
	Quickwriting
	Taking Notes in a Chart
		Younde Goes to Town
		  (A Folktale from Ghana)
		That's Nice
		  by Stephanie Todorovich
		Can We Talk?
		Deaf Donald
		  by Shel Silverstein

Stating Goals
Asking For and Giving Information
Agreeing and Disagreeing
Giving Advice
Describing Future Plans
Suggesting Possibilities
Describing Past Events
Describing a Sequence of Events
	Using Pictures
	Making a K-W-L Chart
	Using Context
	Making a Story Map
	Making a Timeline
	Summarizing
	Quickwriting
		Bouki's Glasses
		  (A Haitian Folktale)
		David Klein
		  by Mel Glenn
		A Biography of Homero E.
		  Acevedo II

Comparing the Past and the
  Present
Identifying Purpose
Making Deductions
Asking "Wh" Questions
Identifying Cause and Effect
Giving Reasons
	Taking Notes in a Chart
	Making a K-W-L Chart
	Reading a Line Graph
	Making a Word Map
	Using Context
		An Immigrant in the United
		  States
		  by Ponn Pet
		The Unexpected Heroine
		  by Glennette Tilley Turney
		The Microscope
		  by Maxine Kumin
		Change
		  by Charlotte Zolotow

Making Guesses
Relating Cause and Effect
Agreeing
Reporting Someone's Ideas
Asking For and Giving Information
  About the Past
Making Comparisons
	Quickwriting
	Using Pictures
	Making a Story Map
	Making a K-W-L Chart
	Taking Notes
	Making a Word Map
		Stewed, Roasted, or Live?
		  (A Chinese Folktale)
		Sharing a Culture
		Law of the Great Peace
		  Adapted by John Bierhorst
		A Kingdom Lost for a Drop
		  of Honey (A Burmese
		  Folktale)

ACKNOWLEDGMENTS

The authors want to thank colleagues, students, and teachers from whom we have learned much and who have offered strong and encouraging support for this project. We thank Chris Foley, Roseanne Mendoza, Nancy Mann, Elaine Leary, and Lisa McLaughlin for their support in the development and production of this project and for weathering with us the storms and challenges of doing something so new. Our expert office staff—Josie Cressman and Sherrie Tindle—provided intelligent and efficient assistance always accompanied by friendship, and we are appreciative. We also want to thank family members—Erin, Dierdre, and Jim Stack; Kevin and Sean O'Brien, and Joel and Tom Reed—for their love and support during this project.

The publisher and authors wish to thank the following teachers who pilot tested the *Making Connections* program. Their valuable feedback on teaching with these materials greatly improved the final product. We are grateful to all of them for their dedication and commitment to teaching with the program in a prepublication format.

Elias S. Andrade and Gudrun Draper
James Monroe High School
North Hills, CA

Nadine Bagel
Benjamin Franklin Middle School
San Francisco, CA

Kate Bamberg
Newcomer High School
San Francisco, CA

Kate Charles
Sycamore Junior High School
Anaheim, CA

Anne Elmkies, Irene Killian, and Kay Stark
Hartford Public Schools
Hartford, CT

Genoveva Goss
Alhambra High School
Alhambra, CA

Margaret Hartman
Lewisville High School
Lewisville, TX

Carmen N. Jimenez
Intermediate School 184
New York, NY

Rob Lamont and Judith D. Clark
Trimble Technical High School
Fort Worth, TX

Judi Levin
Northridge Middle School
Northridge, CA

Ligita Longo
Spring Woods High School
Houston, TX

Mary Makena
Rancho Alamitas High School
Garden Grove, CA

Alexandra M. McHugh
Granby, CT

Beatrice W. Miranda
Leal Middle School
San Antonio, TX

Doris Partan
Longfellow School
Cambridge, MA

Jane Pierce
Douglas MacArthur High School
San Antonio, TX

Cynthia Prindle
Thomas Jefferson High School
San Antonio, TX

Sydney Rodrigues
Doig Intermediate School
Garden Grove, CA

Cecelia Ryan
Monte Vista High School
Spring Valley, CA

Patsy Thompson
Gwinnett Vocational Center
Lawrenceville, GA

Fran Venezia
North Dallas High School
Dallas, TX

The publisher and authors would also like
to thank the following people who reviewed
the *Making Connections* program at various
stages of development. Their insights and
suggestions are much appreciated.

Suzanne Barton
Fort Worth Independent School District
Forth Worth, TX

Keith Buchanan
Fairfax County Public Schools
Fairfax, VA

Carlos Byfield
San Diego City College
San Diego, CA

John Croes
Lowell High School
Lowell, MA

Flo Decker
El Paso, TX

Lynn Dehart
North Dallas High School
Dallas, TX

Cecilia Esquer
El Monte High School
El Monte, CA

Marge Gianelli
Canutillo Independent School District
El Paso, TX

Nora Harris
Harlandale Independent School District
San Antonio, TX

Richard Hurst
Holbrook High School
Holbrook, AZ

Betty J. Mace-Matluck
Southwest Educational Development
   Laboratory
Austin, TX

Jacqueline Moase-Burke
Oakland Independent School District
Oakland, MI

Jeanne Perrin
Boston Public Schools
Boston, MA

Ron Reese
Long Beach Unified School District
Long Beach, CA

Linda Sasser
Alhambra School District
Alhambra, CA

Donna Sievers
Garden Grove Unified School District
Garden Grove, CA

Stephen F. Sloan
James Monroe High School
North Hills, CA

Dorothy Taylor
Adult Learning Center
Buffalo Public Schools
Buffalo, NY

Beth Winningham
James Monroe High School
North Hills, CA

COMPONENTS OF THE MAKING CONNECTIONS PROGRAM

In addition to the student text, each level of Making Connections includes the following components:

Teacher's Extended Edition

This Teacher's Extended Edition provides:

- an introduction to the thematic, integrated teaching approach
- a description of several approaches to presenting literature selections
- a guide to the study strategies that appear in the student book
- detailed teaching suggestions for each activity
- suggestions for extension activities
- listening scripts

Workbooks

Workbooks provide additional practice in using the vocabulary, language functions, language structures, and study strategies introduced in each of the thematic units. Workbook activities can be used in class or assigned as homework.

CD-ROM

This lively, fun, user-friendly program features highly interactive units that parallel the student text. Students engage in sentence completion, interact with videos, create notes from a variety of sources, and complete graphs and charts. Also included is a writing area, an additional language practice section, and printing scorecards for each unit. The program is colorful, easy to navigate and offers a help feature on every screen.

Literacy Masters

Literacy Masters provide special support for preliterate students. These materials are designed for students who enter the program at the Preproduction or Early Production stage. (Students who have only minimal comprehension of English.) The materials correspond with the units of *Making Connections I* and are very useful in multilevel classes.

The Teacher's Guide to the Heinle & Heinle ESL Program

The Heinle & Heinle ESL Program consists of the two series: *Making Connections 1, 2, and 3,* and *Voices in literature, Bronze, Silver, and Gold,* which can be used independently or together. The Teacher's Guide th the Heinle & Heinle ESL Program provides much practical advice and strategies for using the two series together. In this guide, classroom practitioners will learn how to take advantage of the revisitation of terms, themes, content and literature are organized thematically, students can continuously relate and analyze academic concepts and literary works. This Teacher's Guide also offers strategies for providing instruction to students at many levels—from beginning English language proficiency to advanced levels of content-based and literature-based instruction. A technology section describes how instructors can use electronic support, such as e-mail and software, to expand on the activities found in *Making Connections* and *Voices in Literature.*

Assessment Program

The Assessment Program consists of several components and accommodates a range of assessment philosophies and formats. Included are:

- a portfolio assessment kit, complete with a teacher's guide to using portfolios and forms for student and teacher evaluation
- two "progress checks" per unit
- one comprehensive test per unit

Transparencies

Color Transparencies provide enlargements of visuals from the student texts. Many teachers find it helpful to view visuals with the students as they point out details. They may also write on pages using blank overlay transparencies.

Activity Masters

Reproducible activity masters support activities from the student book by providing write-on forms and graphic organizers for student's use. Activities for use with these masters consistently promote active student roles in engaging experiences.

Tape Program

Audio Tapes provide opportunities for group and individual extended practice with the series materials. The tapes contain all the listening activities included in the student texts. Scripts of the recorded material are included in the Teacher's Extended Edition.

MAKING CONNECTIONS 2:

An Integrated Approach to Learning English

▼ How much fat?

▲ What's a healthy diet?

▲ What's good to eat?

◄ May I take your order?

◀ How did the potato get to North America?

CHOOSING FOODS

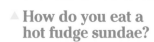

▲ How do you eat a hot fudge sundae?

◀ What's your favorite food?

Language Focus:

Expressing Likes and Dislikes

- I like pizza.
- I love pizza.
- I don't like pretzels.
- I can't stand pretzels.
- I hate pretzels.

MUSTARD

LEMONADE

What's your favorite food?

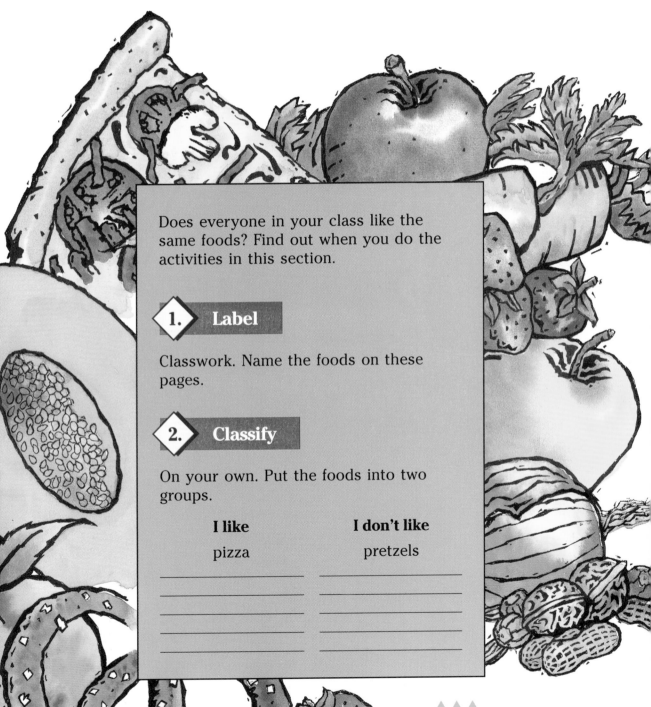

Does everyone in your class like the same foods? Find out when you do the activities in this section.

1. Label

Classwork. Name the foods on these pages.

2. Classify

On your own. Put the foods into two groups.

I like	I don't like
pizza	pretzels
_____	_____
_____	_____
_____	_____
_____	_____

On your own. Find someone who ___likes tacos___. Write the person's name.

Find someone who _____,
a. likes hot dogs _____
b. doesn't like pizza _____
c. hates corn _____
d. loves peanuts _____
e. likes pretzels _____
f. likes carrots for breakfast _____
g. doesn't like strawberries _____
h. _____

4. Shared Reading

Classwork. Listen to the chant. Then chant with the tape.

I'm Hungry!

Pizza, pretzels, popsicles, and peanuts.

I'm hungry. I'm hungry. I'm hungry. I'm hungry.

Apples, peaches, strawberries, and cantaloupe.

I'd like some. I'd like some. I'd like some. I'd like some.

Mustard, ketchup, hamburgers, and hot dogs.

Just a little. Just a little. Just a little. Just a little.

Cabbage, carrots, cucumbers, and onions.

That's enough. That's enough. That's enough. That's enough.

Tacos, tofu, tangerines, and lemonade.

I'm full! I'm full! I'm full!

5. Compare and Contrast

Pairwork. Work with a partner.
Answer the questions in the Venn Diagram.

Study Strategy:

Making a Venn Diagram

Use a Venn Diagram to compare and contrast things.

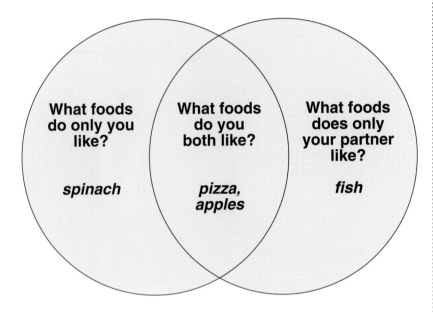

What foods do only you like?

spinach

What foods do you both like?

pizza, apples

What foods does only your partner like?

fish

6. Write

Pairwork. Write a food chant. Use your Venn Diagram for ideas.

7. Shared Reading

Pairwork. Read your chant to the class.

Language Focus:

Comparing Likes

A: I like apples.
B: Me, too.
(So do I.)

A: I really like chicken. Do you?
B: Yes, I do.

May I take your order?

Study Strategy:

Selective Listening

Before listening, ask yourself this question: What information do I need? This helps you listen for the right information.

In this section, you will listen to people ordering food in a restaurant and practice ordering food that you like.

 **1.** **Label**

On your own. Listen and write each customer's order.

 2. **Roleplay**

Pairwork. Practice ordering from this menu.

A: I'd like a chicken sandwich and a small salad, please.

B: For here or to go?

A: For here.

B: Anything to drink?

A: A lemonade, please.

B: What size?

A: Small.

B: Anything else?

A: No, that's all.

B: That'll be $5.05.

ZOE'S DELI

hamburger	1.89
small salad	1.50
large coke	.90
TOTAL	4.29

Language Focus:

Making Polite Requests

- I'd like a tuna fish sandwich, please.
- Could I have a cola and a hamburger, please?

TODAY'S MENU

Chicken sandwich: ....
Salad: ...small $1.50, large............. $2.75
Lemonade: small .80, large............. 2.50

Hamburger: .... .95
Cheeseburger: ....
Soft drinks: ...small .75, large............. 1.89
                                              1.99
French fries .... .90
Fish sandwich .... .75
                                              2.75
Coffee... small .75, large .90
Milk ... small .75, large .90

Write

Groupwork. Write a menu for a restaurant.

4. **Listen Selectively**

On your own. Listen to the dialogues. What are the people going to eat? List the foods.

Dialogue 1

_____
_____
_____

Dialogue 2

_____
_____
_____

Language Focus:

Making and Responding to Suggestions

A: Let's have cheese sandwiches.

B: Good idea. (Sounds good.)

A: What about hot dogs?

B: I don't like hot dogs. What about hamburgers?

5. **Plan**

Groupwork. Plan a picnic for your classmates.

What's good to eat?

What should you eat to stay healthy? You will find out in this section.

1. Label

Classwork. Name the foods in each group.

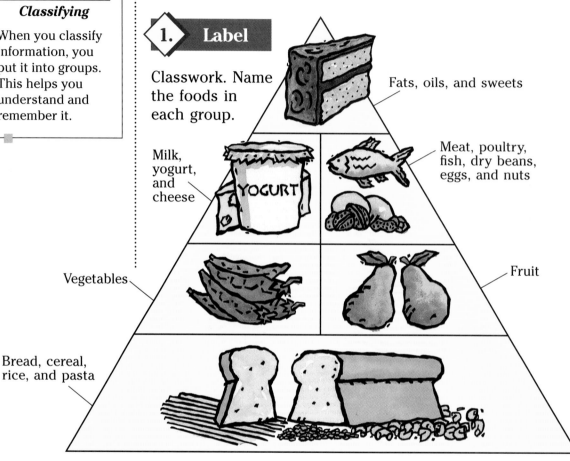

- Fats, oils, and sweets
- Milk, yogurt, and cheese
- Meat, poultry, fish, dry beans, eggs, and nuts
- Vegetables
- Fruit
- Bread, cereal, rice, and pasta

The Food Guide Pyramid classifies foods into six groups. To stay healthy, you need to eat foods from each group.

2. Classify

Pairwork. Reread the food chant on page 2. Group the foods.

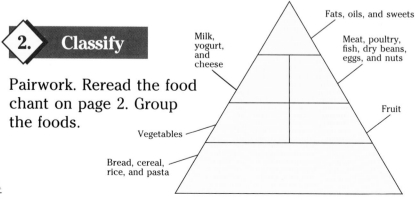

- Milk, yogurt, and cheese
- Fats, oils, and sweets
- Meat, poultry, fish, dry beans, eggs, and nuts
- Fruit
- Vegetables
- Bread, cereal, rice, and pasta

3. ⬦ Identify

Pairwork. How many servings of food do you need daily from each group?

use sparingly

2–3 servings

2–3 servings

3–5 servings

2–4 servings

6–11 servings

Why do you think the Food Guide Pyramid has the shape of a pyramid?

4. ⬦ Measure

Classwork. Your teacher will give you information about serving sizes. Then measure one serving of a food.

Materials: measuring cup, tablespoon, sample foods from each group

one slice
of bread

one cup of raw
leafy greens

one cup of
milk

one egg

one orange

These pictures show one serving of different foods.

5. Measure

Groupwork. Measure a bowl of breakfast cereal.

Materials: box of cereal, milk, bowls, measuring cups

1. How much cereal do you eat for breakfast? Pour this amount in a bowl.
2. Measure the cereal.
3. Read the nutrition label on the cereal box. How large is one serving of this cereal? How many servings of cereal are in your bowl?
4. Measure a half-cup of milk. Pour it on the cereal. Is it too much? Not enough? Just right?
5. How many servings of cereal and milk are in your bowl of cereal?

6. Evaluate

Groupwork. Evaluate Jaime's diet yesterday.

1. Classify the foods. Write them on a Food Guide Pyramid.
2. Write the number of servings next to each food.
3. Count the number of servings in each group.
4. Decide if Jaime ate enough, not enough, or too much food from each group. Write your answers in an evaluation chart.

■ *These pictures show Jaime's meals yesterday.*

Breakfast　　Lunch

Snack

Dinner

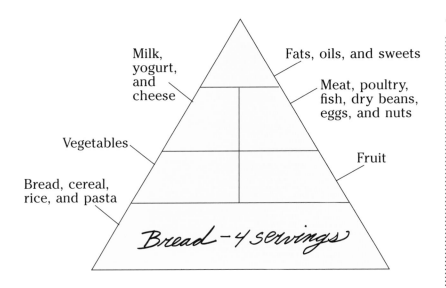

Bread – 4 servings

Evaluation Chart				
Food Group	Number of Servings	Enough	Not Enough	Too Much
Bread...				
Vegetables				
Fruit				
Milk...				
Meat...				
Fats...				

 7. **Self-evaluate**

On your own. Evaluate your diet.

a. List everything you ate yesterday.

b. Classify the foods. Write them on a blank Food Guide Pyramid.

c. Write the number of servings of each food.

d. Count the number of servings in each group.

e. Decide if you ate enough, not enough, or too much food from each group. Write your answers in an evaluation chart.

My Diet Yesterday

Morning:
large bowl of cereal
with milk and
small banana

Afternoon:
tunafish sandwich
green salad
glass of juice
bowl of popcorn

Evening:
tofu with vegetables
bowl of rice and apples
bowl of ice cream (small)

What's a healthy diet?

To stay healthy, it's important to eat different kinds of food. Find out why in this section.

1. **Evaluate**

Classwork. Read and answer the questions.

A healthy diet contains food from different groups in the Food Guide Pyramid. But why do you need to eat different kinds of foods? To answer this question, you need to know about nutrients. You can't see nutrients, but they are the substances in food that keep you healthy. Foods contain different types and amounts of nutrients. No one food has all the nutrients you need. That's why you need to eat different kinds of food.

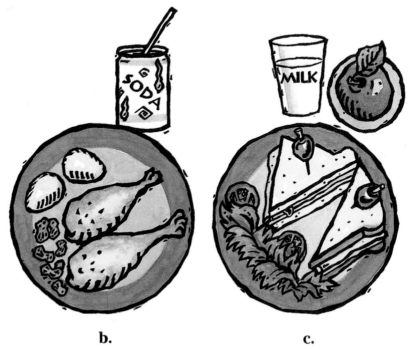

a.

b.

c.

Which lunch shows a healthy diet? Why?

2. Read and Take Notes

On your own. Read for information to complete the chart.

Nutrient Chart		
Nutrient Group	**Function** (What do they do?)	**Good Sources** (What foods?)
Proteins	*help you grow*	*fish, eggs, beans, milk*
Carbohydrates		
Vitamins		
Minerals		
Fats		

Getting the nutrients you need

Nutrients are substances in food that help your body grow and stay healthy. Important nutrients in food are proteins, vitamins, minerals, carbohydrates, and fats. No one food has all the nutrients you need. That's why you need to eat different kinds of food.

Proteins

Your body needs proteins to grow and repair itself. Most foods contain some protein. Meat, fish, nuts, and cheese contain a lot of protein. Cereals and vegetables contain smaller amounts of protein.

77 percent of all American houses have a microwave.

Vitamins and Minerals

Vitamins and minerals help your body work properly. For example, the mineral calcium helps to build bones and teeth. Vitamin A helps your eyes see at night. Most people get enough vitamins and minerals by eating different kinds of food.

Carbohydrates

Carbohydrates give you quick energy. Your body needs this energy to move, grow, and keep warm. Good sources of carbohydrates are bread, rice, corn, fruit, and some vegetables like beets and peas.

56 percent of American families say they eat dinner together every day.

Fats

Fats give you energy, too. Your body can store fat and use it later for energy. Everyone needs some fat in his/her diet. However, too much fat is bad for you. Some foods high in fat are butter, ice cream, sausage, and potato chips.

Your favorite food probably contains more than one kind of nutrient. For example, potatoes contain carbohydrates, vitamins, and minerals. Vegetables contain a lot of vitamins and minerals and some protein. An apple contains carbohydrates and vitamins. By eating different kinds of food, you can get the nutrients you need.

3. Read a Chart

Pairwork. Use your chart on page 13. Practice asking and answering questions.

Q: Which nutrient _____?
A: _____ .

1. helps your body grow
2. helps your body work properly
3. gives you quick energy
4. gives you energy to store

Q: Which food is a good source of _____?
A: _____ .

1. protein	carrots
2. carbohydrate	fish
3. fats	ice cream
4. vitamins and minerals	bread

Language Focus:

Asking and Answering Questions

Q: Which nutrient gives you quick energy?
A: Carbohydrates.

Language Focus:

Asking and Answering Questions

Q: Which food is a good source of protein?
A: Fish.
   Beans.

4. Read a Graph

Groupwork. Study the graph and answer the question below.

This bar graph makes it easy to compare the amount of protein in different foods. Which food has the most protein?

Protein in a Serving of Rice, Beans, and Milk

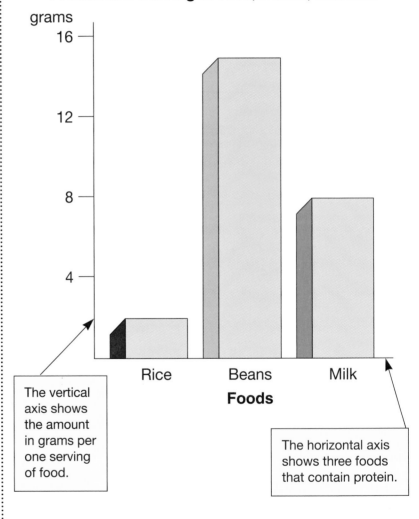

The vertical axis shows the amount in grams per one serving of food.

The horizontal axis shows three foods that contain protein.

5. Make a Graph

Groupwork. Use the labels to make three bar graphs.

Miller's Rice

Nutritional Information
per serving
PROTEIN.........................2 grams
CARBOHYDRATES......21 grams
FAT ....0 grams

DOCTORS
PEANUT BUTTER
NO SALT

Nutritional Information
per serving
PROTEIN.........................9 grams
CARBOHYDRATES........5 grams
FAT ....17 grams

Len's
YOGURT

Nutritional Information
per serving
PROTEIN.....................10 grams
CARBOHYDRATES......14 grams
FAT ....4 grams

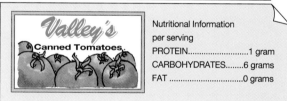

Valley's
Canned Tomatoes

Nutritional Information
per serving
PROTEIN...........................1 gram
CARBOHYDRATES........6 grams
FAT ....0 grams

Protein
Per Serving

grams

| Rice | Peanut Butter | Yogurt | Canned Tomatoes |

Foods

Carbohydrate
Per Serving

grams

| Rice | Peanut Butter | Yogurt | Canned Tomatoes |

Foods

Fat
Per Serving

grams

| Rice | Peanut Butter | Yogurt | Canned Tomatoes |

Foods

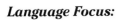

6. Compare and Contrast

Groupwork. Ask questions about the foods on your bar graphs.

Q: Which has _more protein_ , _rice_ or _yogurt_ ?

A: _Yogurt_ .

Nutrient	rice	yogurt
more protein		✓
more carbohydrate		
less fat		

Q: Which food has _the most protein_ ?

A: Yogurt.

Nutrient	rice	yogurt	peanut butter	canned tomatoes
the most protein		✓		
the least protein				
the most carbohydrate				
the least carbohydrate				
the most fat				
the least fat				

7. Synthesize

Classwork. Choose packages of food at home or in a store. Read the labels. Find the amount of protein, carbohydrate, and fat per serving. With your classmates, make three bar graphs. Then compare the nutrients in the different foods.

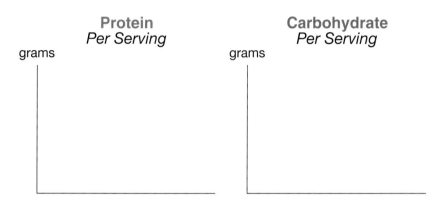

Protein
Per Serving

grams

Foods

Carbohydrate
Per Serving

grams

Foods

Fat
Per Serving

grams

Foods

Americans cook 17 percent of all meals in the microwave.

How much fat?

Too much fat in your diet may be bad for your health. In this section, you will do an investigation to find out which foods contain a lot of fat.

 1. Predict

Classwork. Most nutritionists say that too much fat is bad for your health. Which foods have a lot of fat, some fat, or little or no fat? Make predictions.

Materials: different kinds of food, such as carrots, potato chips, pretzels, potatoes, milk, cheese, butter

A lot of fat	Some fat	Little or no fat
		carrots

 2. Investigate

Groupwork. Follow these steps to test your predictions about the foods in activity 1.

Materials: one brown paper bag, scissors, foods from activity 1

Steps:
1. Cut a brown bag into two-inch squares.
2. Write the name of a food on each square.
3. Rub each food on the square with its name. For liquids, put several drops on the square.
4. Let the squares dry.
5. Hold each square up to a light. Can you see a greasy spot? If so, the food has some fat in it.
6. Paste the squares on a chart. Share your chart with the class.

A lot of fat	Some fat	Little or no fat

Steps:

1.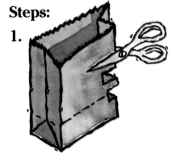

2.

3.

4.

5.

How did the potato get to North America?

Five hundred years ago, potatoes didn't grow in North America, but today they are an important food crop. Where did the potato come from? How did it get to North America? Find out in this section.

1. **Locate**

Classwork. These places were important in the history of the potato. Find them on the map.

- South America
- Andes Mountains
- Colombia

- New England
- Italy
- North America

- Spain
- France
- England

- Portugal
- Ireland

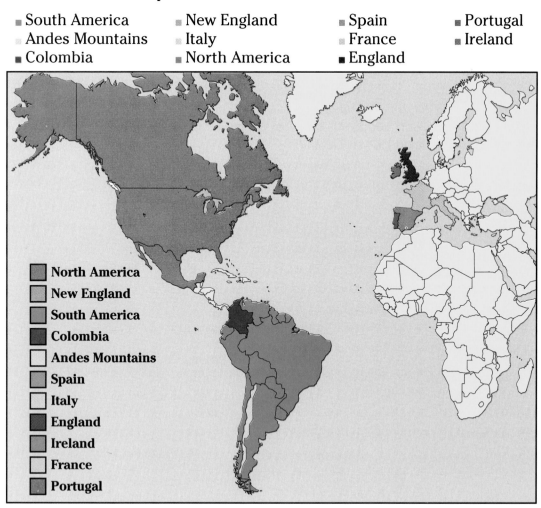

North America
New England
South America
Colombia
Andes Mountains
Spain
Italy
England
Ireland
France
Portugal

2. Shared Reading

How did the potato get to North America?

Five hundred years ago, potatoes grew in the Andes region of South America. They were an important food for the people who lived in these high mountains. In other parts of the world, however, people didn't know about potatoes.

The Spanish invaded South America in the mid-1500s. They learned of potatoes and took some back to Spain. By 1570, white potatoes were growing in parts of Spain. By 1580, people in Portugal and Italy were also growing potatoes.

From Spain, potatoes traveled to France. In France, however, people were afraid to eat this new vegetable. They thought it was poisonous. Louis XVI, the King of France, tried to convince French people to eat potatoes. He even served them at the palace. But for many years, the French still refused to eat potatoes.

Potatoes reached England in a different way. In 1586, the English explorer Sir Francis Drake stopped in Colombia. There he probably picked up some potatoes and took them back to England. At first, the English refused to eat potatoes, too. Instead, they fed them to their pigs and chickens.

From England, the potato traveled to Ireland. The potato grew well in the poor soil of Ireland, and soon it was an important source of nutrients for Irish people.

In the early 1700s, Irish settlers brought the potato to North America. By 1750, many people in New England were growing and eating potatoes.

Digging and harvesting potatoes in Inca times.
—*Poma de Ayola manuscript*

Potato Facts

One hundred and sixty kinds of potatoes are grown in the United States today. Idaho is the biggest producer of potatoes in the United States. About 15 percent of the U.S. potato crop goes into potato chips. Potatoes have no fat. They are good sources of Vitamin C, niacin, and potassium. They are also a good source of carbohydrates.

3. Draw

Pairwork. How did the potato get from South America to North America? Draw its route. Use the map on page 21.

4. Draw Inferences

Pairwork. Who said it—someone from Spain, France, or England? Match the statement on the left with the country on the right.

Circle your answer.
1. "You can't eat that. It might kill you."   a. Spain
2. "I won't eat it. Give it to the animals."   b. France
3. "I'll try it."   c. England

The average time an American family spends eating dinner is 32 minutes.

5. Design

Pairwork. Choose one activity.

a. Help Louis XVI. Think of a way to convince people in France to eat potatoes.
b. Think of a food you like. Design a poster or advertisement to get your classmates to try this food.

How do you eat a hot fudge sundae?

When you look at a hot fudge sundae, you might see ice cream and hot fudge sauce. But when you read a poem about a hot fudge sundae, you might see something else—something very different. Find out what it is in this section.

1. Report

Classwork. Have you ever eaten a hot fudge sundae? What part did you like best?

2. Compare

Classwork. The poet Jonathan Holden looks at a hot fudge sundae and sees the world. What do you see when you look at the parts of a hot fudge sundae?

The whipped cream is like the clouds in the sky.

The _____ is like the _____.

clouds

ground

whipped cream

hot fudge sauce

ice cream

strata

3. **Shared Reading**

Listen to this poem. Then read it aloud several times.

How to Eat a Hot Fudge Sundae

Start with the
clouds. Eat
the clouds. Eat through
to the ground. Eat
the ground until you tap
the first rich vein. Delve
from strata to strata
down to the cold lava
core. Stir
the lava, pick up
the whole goblet, drink
straight from the goblet
until you've finished the world.

—*Jonathan Holden*

4. **Identify**

Pairwork. What words does the poet use to describe the parts of a hot fudge sundae?

whipped cream   _____*clouds*_____

ice cream   _____

hot fudge sauce   _____

5. **Write**

On your own.

1. Choose a food you like. Describe it.

   What shape is it?   round, thin, flat
   What color is it?   red

2. Ask a partner to use your words to draw a picture of something that is not a food.

3. Use your words and your partner's idea to write a poem.

Name of food: PIZZA

Descriptive word: round, thin, red, flat,

Partner idea: Like a spaceship

Activity Menu

Choose one of the following activities to do.

1. Make a Food Display
Cut pictures of food from different magazines. Paste the foods into the correct groups in a Food Guide Pyramid. Then label the foods and display your pyramid.

2. Check Out a Vending Machine
Find a vending machine in your area. List the foods in the vending machine. Write the foods in the correct groups in a food guide pyramid. Does the vending machine provide food from all groups? Report what you learned to the class.

3. What's the Difference?
Take a trip to the grocery store and read some food labels. Compare the amount of fat, protein, and carbohydrate in a serving of these foods. Tell your classmates what you learned.

- whole milk, lowfat milk, and skim milk
- regular yogurt and nonfat light yogurt
- ice cream, sherbet, and ice milk
- butter and margarine
- cottage cheese and cream cheese

4. Supermarket Smarts
Predict answers to the questions below. Then visit a supermarket to check your predictions.

1. How many kinds of breakfast cereal can you buy in a supermarket?
2. How many kinds of fruit are available?
3. What kinds of foods are next to the cash register?
4. What international foods are available?

5. A Meal in a Sandwich

Invent a new kind of sandwich with food from all groups in the Food Guide Pyramid. Give your sandwich a name. Draw or cut pictures of the food in your sandwich. Then make a poster to advertise your sandwich. Include the name of your sandwich on the poster.

6. What's for Lunch?

Can you find these foods in the school cafeteria?
- a food that is high in protein but low in fat
- a food that is high in fat
- a food that costs less than 50 cents
- the cheapest source of carbohydrate
- the most expensive source of protein
- the sweetest food

7. Eating Around the World

Tell your classmates about the food in your native country.
Describe what people eat on a typical day. Present this information to your classmates in a short oral report or on a small poster with pictures.

8. Make a Food Database

Collect data on the nutrients in a variety of foods. Then follow your teacher's instructions to make a food database. Use your database to evaluate your diet or to plan healthy meals.

9. You Are the Chef

Choose a favorite dish. Tell your classmates how to make this dish. List the ingredients and write the instructions. Exchange instructions with a classmate. At home, follow the instructions to make this dish. Bring the food to class and share it with your classmates.

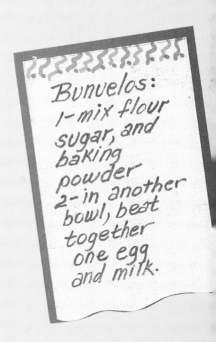

10. Food Customs

People in different parts of the world learn different table manners, or polite ways to eat. Tell about table manners in your native country. List things you should and shouldn't do at a meal. Then interview someone from the United States. Find out what they think you should and shouldn't do at the dinner table. Here are a few questions to get you started:

- *Is it polite to eat everything on your plate or in your dish?*
- *Is it polite to eat with your hands?*

Read on...

How to Eat a Poem

Don't be polite,
Bite in.
Pick it up with your fingers and lick the juice that
    may run down your chin.
It is ready and ripe now, whenever you are.

You do not need a knife or fork or spoon
or plate or napkin or tablecloth.

For there is no core
or stem
or rind
or pit
or seed
or skin
to throw away.

   —*Eve Merriam*

Watermelons

Green Buddhas
On the fruit stand
We eat the smile
and spit out the teeth.

   —*Charles Simic*

95 percent of American families say they ate their last dinner at home.

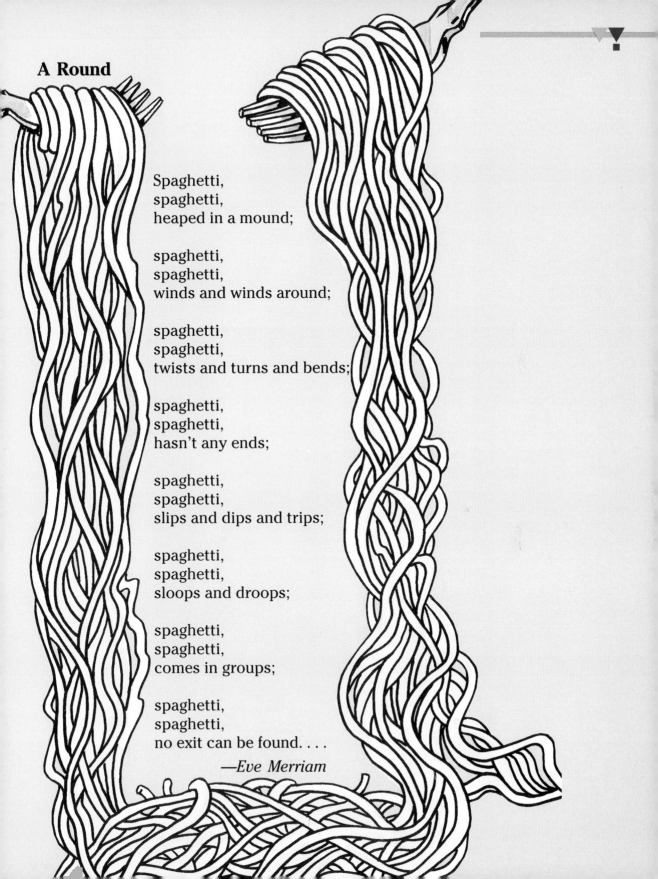

A Round

Spaghetti,
spaghetti,
heaped in a mound;

spaghetti,
spaghetti,
winds and winds around;

spaghetti,
spaghetti,
twists and turns and bends;

spaghetti,
spaghetti,
hasn't any ends;

spaghetti,
spaghetti,
slips and dips and trips;

spaghetti,
spaghetti,
sloops and droops;

spaghetti,
spaghetti,
comes in groups;

spaghetti,
spaghetti,
no exit can be found. . . .

—*Eve Merriam*

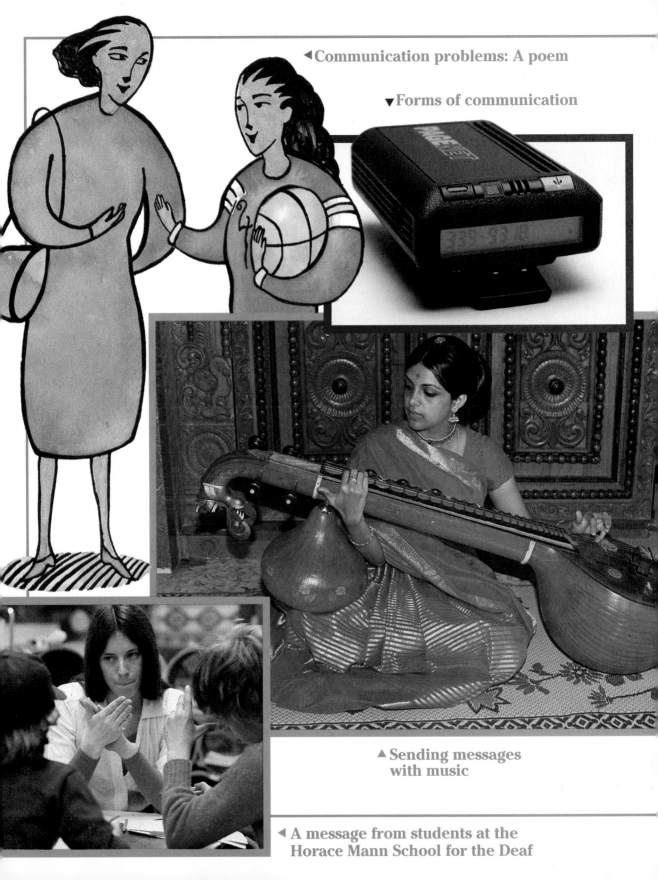

◀ Communication problems: A poem

▼ Forms of communication

▲ Sending messages
with music

◀ A message from students at the
Horace Mann School for the Deaf

▼ Communication problems: A folktale

SENDING MESSAGES

▲ Making sounds: An investigation

Nonverbal communication ▶

Forms of communication

In this section, you will explore ways that people communicate.

1. Identify

Classwork. What are some ways that people communicate?

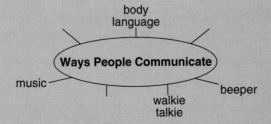

body language

Ways People Communicate

music

beeper

walkie talkie

2. Evaluate

Pairwork. Choose one form of communication and write about it in a chart.

Form of Communication: _telephone_	
Advantages +	**Disadvantages** −
You can talk to someone far away.	It costs money.
You don't have to leave home.	You can't see the person.

Nonverbal communication

In this section, you will investigate ways that people communicate without using words.

1. Identify

Classwork. What do these symbols mean?

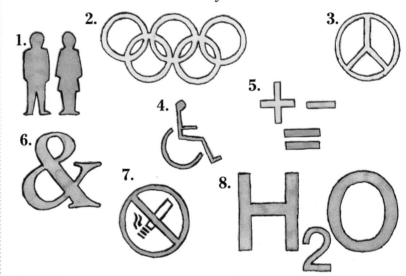

Symbols communicate important information.

2. Design

Groupwork. Design a symbol to communicate information. Choose one of these ideas, or think of your own.

You must wear shoes here.

This is an ESL classroom.

Don't put bottles in this trash can.

No eating here.

Friendship.

Love.

Danger.

Language Focus:

Asking What Something Means

Q: What does this symbol mean?

A: It means "you can't smoke here."

3. Match

Classwork. What information are these people communicating? Match the people with the ideas on the right.

Body language communicates important information.

I have a question.
Look at that.
I'm angry.
Hi!
I'm sad.
Come here.
I'm worried.
It's this big.
I don't know.

4. Compare and Contrast

Pairwork. Take turns using body language to communicate these ideas.

Did you use the same body language?

	YES	NO
1. I'm tired.	_____	✓
2. I'm happy.	_____	_____
3. I understand.	_____	_____
4. I'm listening.	_____	_____
5. Goodbye.	_____	_____
6. That smells bad.	_____	_____
7. Yes.	_____	_____
8. No.	_____	_____

Tell your classmates if you used the same or different body language.

5. Draw

Pairwork. Draw three faces. Use the mouth, eyes, and eyebrows in each row below. Then tell what information each person is communicating.

Example:  *Artists use special techniques to show the body language of cartoon characters.*

Row	Information	Eyebrows	Eyes	Mouth
1	*I'm angry*	‿⌣	♂ ♂	⌒
2	_____	⌒⌒	⊙⊙	⌣
3	_____	⌒⌒	♂♂	⊏⊐
4	_____	⌒⌒	⊙⊙	◡

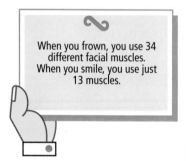

When you frown, you use 34 different facial muscles. When you smile, you use just 13 muscles.

Communication problems: Younde Goes to Town (a folktale)

In this section, you will read a story about a man named Younde. When Younde travels to a faraway town, he meets people who speak a different language. Younde can't understand their language, and they can't understand his language. You can imagine the kinds of problems he has.

1. Think-Pair-Share

a. Think about a time when you didn't understand someone.
- Where were you?
- What did you do?
- How did you feel?

b. Tell your story to a partner. Listen carefully to your partner's story.

c. Get together with another pair. Tell your partner's story.

2. Learn New Words

Classwork. Study the pictures and captions on pages 38–40. Use information in the pictures to define these words:

Picture #1: village ___*a small town*___

Picture #2: donkey _____

Picture #3: herd _____

Picture #4: tremendous _____

Picture #5: unusual _____

Picture #6: funeral procession _____

> **Study Strategy:**
> **Using Pictures**
> Pictures can help you understand a story and learn new words.

3. **Preview**

Classwork. Use the pictures and captions on pages 38–40 to answer the questions in a Know/Want to Know chart.

Answer these questions before you read the story.

Answer this question after you read the story.

Know	Want to know	Learned
What do you know about the story from the pictures?	What do you want to know?	What did you learn?
Younde lives in a village.	*Where is the village?*	

Study Strategy:

Making a Know/ Want to Know Chart

Making a Know/ Want to Know chart is a good way to get ready to read.

4. **Shared Reading**

Background

Younde Goes to Town is a folktale from Ghana, West Africa. Folktales are stories told aloud by each generation to the next.

Younde Goes to Town

Once in the country of Akim, in the hills far from the coast, there was a man named Younde. He was a simple man who farmed and hunted like the other people in his village. He often heard about the big town of Accra by the ocean, but he had never seen it. He had never been farther from his village than the river.

Younde was a farmer. He lived in a village in the hills.

But one day Younde had to go to Accra. He put on his best clothes and took his knife and put it in his belt. He wrapped some food in a cloth and put it on his head and started out. He walked for many days, and the road was hot and dusty. After a while, he was out of his own country, and people didn't speak his language any more. He came closer and closer to Accra. There were many people and donkeys on the road, all going to town or coming back from town.

Then he saw a large herd of cows grazing by the edge of the road. He had never seen so many cows in his life. He stopped and looked at them in wonder. There was a little boy herding the cows, and he went up to him and asked, "Who is the owner of these cows?"

But the boy didn't understand because Younde spoke Akim and the boy knew only the Ga language. So the boy replied, "Minu," which meant "I don't understand" in the Ga language.

"Minu! What a rich man he must be to have so many cows!" Younde said.

He continued his way into the town. He was very impressed with everything he saw.

He came to a large building and stopped to look at it. It was made of stone, and it was very high. When a woman came by, Younde spoke to her.

"What a tremendous house!" he said. "What rich person can own such a building?"

But the woman didn't understand Younde because he spoke Akim and she spoke the Ga language. So she replied to him:

"Minu," which meant "I don't understand" in the Ga language.

"Minu! That man again!" said Younde.

Younde was overcome. No one in his village was as wealthy as Minu. As he went farther into town, he saw more wonders. He came to the market. It covered a space larger than all the houses in Younde's village. He walked through the market and saw women selling things that were rare in his village, like iron pots and iron spoons.

One day Younde took a trip to the big town of Accra. There were many people and donkeys on the road.

On the road to Accra, Younde met a boy with a large herd of cows.

Near Accra, he saw a tremendous house.

Younde went to the market in Accra. There he saw many unusual things.

"Where do all these things come from?" Younde asked a little girl.

She smiled at him.

"Minu," she replied.

Younde was silent. Everything was Minu. Minu everywhere.

Younde finished his business in Accra, wrapped food in his cloth and started home. When he came to the edge of town, he saw a great procession and he heard the beating of drums. He came close and saw it was a funeral. Men were carrying a coffin and women were crying.

"Who is this person who has died?" Younde asked one of the men.

"Minu," the man answered.

"What! The great Minu is dead?" Younde said. "Oh, poor Minu! He had to leave all his wealth behind. He has died just like an ordinary person!"

Younde continued home, but he couldn't get the tragedy of Minu from his mind.

"Poor Minu!" he said over and over again. "Poor Minu!"

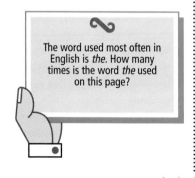

The word used most often in English is *the*. How many times is the word *the* used on this page?

On his way home, Younde saw a funeral procession.

5. Role Play

a. Pairwork. Choose one of these characters from the story. Find the conversation between Younde and this character in the story. Write it as a dialogue.

Characters: *woman*   *little girl*   *man*

Example:

Younde:	*Who is the owner of all these cows?*
Little boy:	*Minu.*
Younde:	*Minu! What a rich man he must be to have so many cows!*

b. Pairwork. Practice reading the dialogue aloud.

c. Pairwork. Share ideas about the story with your partner. Here are some questions you might think about:

- Did you like the story? Why or why not?
- Why did Younde have a communication problem?
- Younde didn't understand the word *Minu.* What did he think it meant? What did it really mean?

6. Classify

On your own. Find words in the story to answer the questions.

What did Younde see?	What did Younde hear?	How did Younde feel?
donkeys	*Ga language*	*impressed*

> **Study Strategy:**
>
> **Classifying**
>
> Classifying, or grouping, words helps you to learn and remember them.

7. Make a Chart

Pairwork. In the story, Younde talked to four people. Write about these people in a chart.

	(1) little boy	(2) woman	(3) little girl	(4) man
Where was the person?	*near the road*			
What was the person doing?	*taking care of cows*			
What did Younde ask?	*"Who is the owner of these cows?"*			
What did the person answer?	*"Minu."*			
What did Younde think?	*Minu owned all of the cows.*			

Use the chart to retell the story.

8. Write

a. Classwork. Use the information in this chart to tell about another person Younde met.

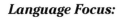

	Person: _an old man_
Where was the person?	*in the market*
What was the person doing?	*selling donkeys*
What did Younde ask?	*"Who owns all these donkeys?"*
What did the person answer?	*"Minu."*
What did Younde think?	*Minu owned all of the donkeys.*

Language Focus:

Asking for Information

- Where was the person?
- What was the person doing?
- What did Younde ask?
- What did the person answer?
- What did Younde think?

b. Add quotation marks to each speaker's words in this new scene from the story.

In the market, Younde saw an old man selling donkeys. The man had large donkeys and small donkeys. He had more donkeys than there were in the whole village of Akim.

Who owns all these donkeys? Younde asked the man.

Minu, said the man.

Really? Minu owns all of these donkeys? Younde asked.

c. Pairwork. Imagine another person Younde met. Write your ideas in a chart.

	Person: _____
Where was the person?	
What was the person doing?	
What did Younde ask?	
What did the person answer?	
What did Younde think?	

d. Pairwork. Use the ideas in your chart to write a new scene for the story. Then share your scene with the class.

Language Focus:

Using Quotation Marks in Reporting What Someone Said

- "Where do all of these things come from?" Younde asked a little girl.
- "What a tremendous house!" Younde said.

There are about 490,000 words in the English language.

Communication problems: That's Nice (a poem)

Sometimes people don't listen when you talk to them. This is just what happens in the poem *That's Nice*.

 1. Quickwrite

On your own. Write about a time when someone didn't listen to you. What happened? How did you feel?

 2. Shared Reading

Pairwork. Listen to the poem. Then take turns reading a line.

That's Nice

I made the team!
Really?
Yes, and I'm the youngest player.
That's nice. Did you clean your room?
Yes. The coach said I'm the fastest on the team.
Is your homework done?
No, I thought I'd shoot some baskets first—
to practice.
Practice what?

—*Stephanie Todorovich*

Share Ideas

Classwork. What's your reaction to the poem? Share ideas with your classmates and teacher. Here are some other questions to think about:

a. Do you think the two people have a communication problem? Why or why not?

b. How do you think the basketball player feels at the beginning of the conversation? At the end? Why?

c. What questions would you ask the basketball player?

 Sequence

Pairwork. Put the lines in this conversation in the correct order. Then read the conversation aloud.

____ Next month.
____ Do you know anyone on the Baylor team?
____ Who are you going to play on the 15th?
____ That's wonderful! When's your first game?
_1_ I made the team!
____ No, I don't.
____ On the 15th.
____ The team from Baylor High School.
____ What day next month?

What words helped you to know the order of lines in the dialogue?
Do these two people have a communication problem? Why or why not?

5. Question and Answer

Pairwork. Follow these steps to practice having a conversation.

a. Write this question on a piece of paper.

What did you do last weekend?

b. Give your paper to a partner. Your partner answers the question on the paper.

What did you do last weekend?
I went to the movies.
What did you see?

c. Read your partner's answer. Write a question about the answer.

d. How long can you continue the conversation? Try to fill up the page.

e. Change partners. Try the activity again, but this time try talking instead of writing.

6. Write

a. Groupwork. Who said it? Match these quotes with
the people in the pictures.

"I failed the test," _she said to her friend._

"Mom, I aced the test," _____

"Do you want another hamburger?" _____

"Look at that grasshopper!" _____

"That was a great game!" _____

Two friends

Two friends

Mother and daughter

Teacher and female student

Boyfriend and girlfriend

b. Choose one of the quotes. Continue the
conversation. Write your ideas.

c. Share your conversation with another group.

Making sounds

You hear a sound when something vibrates or moves back and forth. In this section, you will investigate vibrations and the sounds they produce.

 Predict

Groupwork. Study these pictures and answer the questions in the chart.

When you pluck a rubber band, it vibrates or moves back and forth. These vibrations produce sounds.

A

B

C

	Prediction	Actual
Which rubber band vibrates faster?	A or B	A or B
Which vibrations produce a higher sound?	A or B	A or B
Which rubber band vibrates faster?	A or C	A or C
Which vibrations produce a higher sound?	A or C	A or C

2. Investigate

Groupwork. Follow these steps to test your predictions.

Materials: a book, a large rubber band, two pencils

Steps:

1. Put the rubber band around the book.

2. Put a pencil under the rubber band on each side of the book.

3. Pluck the rubber band in the middle. Listen to the sound it makes.

4. Use one hand to stretch the rubber band just a little. Pluck it with the other hand.
   - Does the rubber band make a higher or lower sound than before?
   - Is the rubber band tighter or looser than before?
   - Does the rubber band vibrate more quickly or more slowly than before?

5. Release the rubber band. Pluck it in the middle again. Listen to the sound again.

6. Press down on the middle of the rubber band. Pluck the rubber band on one side of your finger.
   - Does the rubber band make a higher or lower sound than before? _____
   - Is the part of the rubber band that vibrates shorter or longer than before? _____
   - Does the rubber band vibrate more quickly or more slowly than before? _____

7. Record the results of your investigation in the chart in Activity 1.

Steps:

1. 2.

3.

4.

5.

6.

3. Synthesize

Groupwork. Tell what you learned from this investigation.

1. When you (tighten/loosen) the rubber band, it vibrates (more quickly/more slowly).
2. When you (tighten/loosen) the rubber band, you hear a (higher/lower) sound.
3. When you (shorten/lengthen) the rubber band, it vibrates (more quickly/more slowly).
4. When you (shorten/lengthen) the rubber band, you hear a (higher/lower) sound.
5. When the rubber band vibrates (quickly/slowly), you hear a (high/low) sound.

4. Apply

Groupwork. Read the information below and answer the question.

A guitar is a musical instrument made with stretched strings and a sounding box. The strings and the sounding box vibrate to produce sounds.

Strings

The sounding box

How can you make high notes and low notes on a guitar?

Language Focus:

Describing Cause and Effect

- When you pluck the rubber band, it vibrates.
- When the rubber band vibrates, you hear a sound.

Answer to Activity 4: To make high and low notes, you can tighten and loosen the strings on a guitar. You can also use your fingers to make the strings shorter or longer.

Sending messages with music

Music is an important form of communication. In this section, you will read about different kinds of musical instruments and how they make sounds.

 1. Quickwrite

On your own. Listen to this music. What does it make you think of? How does it make you feel? As you listen, write your ideas.

 2. Preview

Groupwork. Study the pictures on pages 52–53. Then read the questions below and write your guesses.

What vibrates when you play a violin?

Our Guess	Text Information
_____	_____

What vibrates when you play a flute?

Our Guess	Text Information
_____	_____

What vibrates when you play a drum?

Our Guess	Text Information
_____	_____

Dolphins and bats can make sounds that are more than 100 times higher than a person can make. These sounds are so high that people can't hear them.

Read or listen to check your guesses.

Making Music

A guitar is called a stringed musical instrument because it is made with strings stretched over a sounding box. Both the strings and the sounding box vibrate when the strings are plucked. Musicians know just how tense and how long to make the different-sized strings in order to create the high notes and low notes, or the pitch of music. Other stringed instruments include the violin, piano, and ukulele.

Violin   **Piano**   **Ukulele**

Wind instruments make musical sounds in a different way. A wind instrument is basically a hollow tube with a mouthpiece. When a musician blows into the mouthpiece, the air inside the tube vibrates. The length of vibrating air inside the tube is called the air column. By changing the size of the air column, the musician can make high and low notes. For example, making the air column shorter produces higher notes. Pipe organs, flutes, bugles, and saxophones are different kinds of wind instruments. They all depend upon vibrating air columns for their sounds.

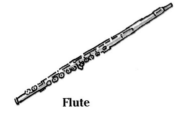

Flute   **Pipe organ**

Drums of different sizes and shapes are still another kind of musical instrument. Hitting a thin surface of a drum causes the surface to vibrate and produce sound. Hitting a drum hard makes a loud sound. Hitting it lightly makes soft sounds.

Drum

4. **Take Notes in a Chart**

Pairwork. Look back at the reading and take notes in a chart.

Study Strategy:

Taking Notes in a Chart

When you take notes, write only the most important words.

Paragraph	Main Idea	Details and Examples
#1	the strings and sounding box vibrate on a stringed instrument	violin, piano, ukulele
#2		
#3		

Language Focus:

**Asking for
and Giving
Information**

Q: What vibrates
when you play
a violin?

A: The strings and
sounding box.

5. **Test Your Knowledge**

Pairwork. Use the chart to practice asking and
answering questions.

Example: What vibrates when you play __a violin__ ?

 __The strings and sounding box.__

6. **Match** 🎞️

a. On your own. Match the causes on the left with the
effects on the right. Use one effect twice.

CAUSE	EFFECT
1. When you play a stringed instrument,	a. they vibrate.
2. When you play a saxophone,	b. it vibrates.
3. When you pluck the strings on a guitar,	c. it makes soft sounds.
4. When you hit the surface of a drum,	d. the strings and sounding box vibrate.
5. When you hit a drum lightly,	e. the air column vibrates.
6. When you play a piano,	

b. Compare answers with a classmate.

▲▲▲

7. Apply

a. Groupwork. How do these instruments make sounds? What vibrates? Write your ideas in a chart.

Instrument	What Vibrates?
maracas	_____
'ud	_____
fujara	_____
sistrum	_____
sitar	_____
horn	_____

b. Share your group's ideas with the class.

◀ Turkish 'ud

▼ Tibetan horn

▲ Slovakian fujara

▲ Indian sitar

▲ South American maracas

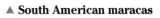

People who can't hear have special ways to communicate. In this section, you will read about some of these special ways.

1. List

Classwork. Read the question below and list your answers.

The students at the Horace Mann School for the Deaf in Allston, Massachusetts wrote the articles on the following pages. How do you think students at this school communicate?

2. Match

Groupwork. Match these gestures with the words on the left.

Many hearing-impaired (deaf) people use sign language to communicate. This language uses gestures instead of speech. Some signs look like what they represent. Others do not.

hello	watch
bird	flower
police officer	flag

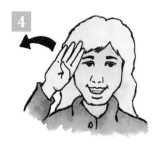

4

5

6

Answers to Activity 2: 1. Police Officer; 2. Bird; 3. Watch;
4. Hello; 5. Flag; 6. Flower.

 3. **Speculate**

Pairwork. How do these devices help hearing-impaired people to communicate? Writer your guesses in a chart.

These special devices help hearing-impaired people to communicate.

TDD

Closed-caption decoder

Vibrating clock

Device	My Guess	Text Information
TDD	_____	_____
	_____	_____
Closed-caption decoder		
	_____	_____
Vibrating clock	_____	_____

Read this article. Add information to the chart on page 57.

Devices That Help the Deaf

How does a deaf person know when his doorbell is ringing or when someone is calling her on the phone? Can a deaf person watch television? Wake up with an alarm clock? A hearing person can do all of these, but deaf people need special devices to help them.

Most hearing children don't know about the little tricks deaf people use. Here's a description of some of them.

A TDD, or a Telecommunication Device for the Deaf, helps deaf people talk on the telephone. When the phone rings, a light flashes. The person picks up the phone, puts on the TDD, and types and reads the conversation. Doorbells that flash a light when someone pushes the bell are also popular.

A closed-caption decoder makes it possible for a deaf person to watch TV. Many shows are closed-captioned for the hearing impaired. Words appear at the bottom of the screen and the person reads what's being said.

Hate waking up to a blaring alarm? Deaf people use vibrating clocks. The alarm shakes the pillow. It feels like an earthquake, but it makes us jump out of bed!

All of these devices help deaf people. There are many others that deaf people use at home, school, and work.

—By students at the Horace Mann School for the Deaf

5. Identify

Pairwork. Identify these devices.

a. When a hearing-impaired person turns on this device, he or she can read a telephone conversation.
What is this device? _____

b. When this device goes off, it shakes the pillow.
What is this device? _____

c. When someone pushes this device, a light flashes.
What is it? _____

d. When you turn on this device, words appear on a TV screen.
What is it? _____

6. Design

Groupwork. These devices help hearing people to communicate. Redesign one of these devices for hearing-impaired people to use.

When someone wants to talk to you, they can call your beeper. When they dial your number, your beeper makes a noise. This tells you to call your home or office for a message.

Many buildings have smoke alarms. When there is a fire, the smoke causes a bell to ring. The bell warns you to leave the building.

Cars have horns. When the driver presses the horn, it makes a noise.

With a baby monitor, parents can sit in another room and hear every sound in the baby's room.

You can attach an answering machine to your telephone. When someone calls you, the answering machine records their message. When you get home, you can listen to the messages.

Language Focus:

Stating an Opinion

- We think hearing people should learn sign language.

- We don't think hearing people should learn sign language.

7. State an Opinion

Groupwork. Many deaf people use sign language to communicate. Do you think hearing people should learn sign language, too? Why or why not?

Opinion: _____

Reasons: _____

_____

_____

An editorial is a special kind of newspaper article. It states the author's opinion about something. In this editorial, students from the Horace Mann School for the Deaf give opinions about learning sign language.

Teaching Sign Language in Schools

We think hearing people should learn sign language as a separate class in school. Why? So that some day soon, all people in our country will be able to talk with deaf people.

If hearing people learned sign language, it would be easier for deaf people to communicate. We could communicate better with waiters in restaurants, clerks in stores, doctors, even hearing kids on the playgrounds.

Hearing people would quickly see the benefits. The most important is that they could make friends with deaf people. Many hearing people who know sign language say they like to sign with deaf kids and adults.

We know many hearing people who are curious to learn sign language. In the future, if more hearing people knew sign, maybe a hearing person could become an interpreter for the deaf world.

We recommend that all schools offer sign language as an option for their students. It would make a big difference for all people.

—By students at the Horace Mann School for the Deaf

9. Take Notes

Groupwork. Look back at each paragraph in the reading and take notes in a chart.

Title: Teaching Sign Language in School	
Paragraph 1 Introduction	What is the opinion of students at the Horace Mann School for the Deaf?
Paragraph 2	What is their first reason?
Paragraph 3	What is their second reason?
Paragraph 4	What is their third reason?
Paragraph 5 Conclusion	What do they say again?

Language Focus:

Giving Reasons

- If hearing people learned sign language, it would be easier for deaf people to communicate.
- If hearing people learned sign language, deaf people could communicate more easily.

10. Write

Groupwork. Follow these steps to write an editorial for your classmates to read.

a. What should students learn at school? Brainstorm a list of ideas.

What should students learn at school?
to speak a foreign language
to play a musical instrument
history of different countries

b. Choose one idea on your list. Think of reasons to support your opinion. Write your ideas on a tree diagram.

Students should learn to speak a foreign language

— They could help visitors in the U.S.

— They could read books in other languages.

— They could watch foreign movies without subtitles.

— They could speak to people from different countries.

c. Organize your ideas in a chart. In box 1, write your opinion. In boxes 2–4, write your best reasons. In box 5, restate your opinion.

Title: _____

1. Introduction

We think students should learn _____ at school.

2. Reason

3. Reason

4. Reason

5. Conclusion

d. Use your chart to write an editorial for your classmates to read.

Activity Menu

Choose one of the following activities to do.

1. Identify Body Language
Collect pictures of people using body language. Take photographs or cut pictures from magazines. Post your pictures on a classroom wall and ask your classmates to tell what information the body language communicates.

2. Make a Display
Choose a phrase that describes an emotion, such as *I'm sad* or *I love you*. See how many ways you can communicate this idea. Translate it into other languages. Use symbols or music. Find or write poetry. Share the results of your investigation.

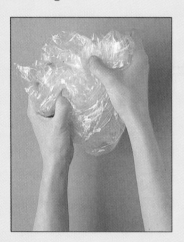

3. Look for Symbols
Look for symbols around your school and neighborhood. Photograph or draw each symbol. Write a caption for each symbol telling what it means. Use your pictures and captions to make a wall display.

4. Create Sound Effects
Storytellers use sound effects to make a story seem more real. For example, to make the sound of a fire, you can crumple a plastic wrapper. To make the sound of waves on the shore, you can put dried peas in a metal bowl and slowly roll the bowl back and forth.

Reread the story *Younde Goes to Town*. What sounds do you hear in the story? Find a way to make these sounds and then tell the story with your sound effects.

5. Play a Musical Scale
Materials: large and small drinking glasses, water, pencil.
Put different amounts of water into each glass. Using the pencil, gently strike each glass near the top. The tone that you hear depends on the length of the water column in the glass. Adjust the amount of water in the glasses so that you can play a musical scale. Then figure out a way to write down a song for this instrument.

6. Greeting Card Messages

Some people use greeting cards to send messages. You can find these cards in a drugstore or stationary store. Do a survey of greeting cards in a nearby store to find answers to these questions:

- What categories or groups of greeting cards does the store have?
- Which category of cards has the largest selection?
- How are the cards alike? Different?
- Which card do you like best? Why?

7. A Clothing Message

Choose pictures of people wearing different types of clothing. What information does their clothing communicate? Is it possible to get an incorrect message from clothing? Give an example.

8. Research a Communication Device

Choose a communication device that interests you. Look for information about this device in the library. Find out its history and how it works. Tell your classmates what you learned.

9. Investigate Map Symbols

Study a map of your area. Make a list of the symbols used on your map. Look at the map legend to learn the meaning of each symbol. Present the results of your research to the class.

10. Study Animal Communication

Choose an animal to observe. What sounds does it make? What body language does it use? Draw a picture of the animal and write down your observations. Then write a summary of your ideas, telling how this animal communicates. Present your ideas to the class.

Read on . . .

Can We Talk?

It may not be your typical typewriter. But it's just the right type, for a dolphin.

Researchers at Walt Disneyworld's EPCOT Center have designed a giant "typewriter" for Toby and Bob, two bottlenose dolphins. With it, they hope to be able to communicate with the two animals.

The typewriter is the same size as a minivan. It has 60 "keys" that are actually hollow tubes. Each tube is labeled with a different 3-D symbol. When the dolphin pokes its snout into that tube, it triggers a response.

For example, if Toby chooses symbols for "Give stick to Toby," the trainers will offer the stick. Toby can use it to open a container holding food or toys.

The trainers hope Toby and Bob will learn word symbols in a year. After that, they want to train the duo to string words together to form sentences.

So who knows? Maybe one day you'll see these dolphins in a . . . secretary pool!

Deaf Donald

Deaf Donald met Talkie Sue

But  was all he could do.

And Sue said, "Donald, I sure do like you."

But  was all he could do.

And Sue asked Donald, "Do you like me too?"

But  was all he could do.

"Goodbye then, Donald, I'm leaving you."

But  was all he did do.

And she left forever so she never knew

That  means I love you.
　　　　　　　　　　　　　　　—Shel Silverstein

▲ Reaching your goals: A song

▲ What are your goals? ▶

▲ Reaching your
goals: A folktale ▶

▲ Career goals

SETTING GOALS

▼ Goals of the U.S. government

Liliana DaSilva is a junior in high school.

I plan to go to college after high school. I want to work as a computer programmer after college. Someday I'd like to travel around the world.

François Cerneus is a high school sophomore.

I want to get good grades in school this year. I would also like to become a good basketball player. I hope to become a doctor. Someday I'd like to get married and have a family.

What are your goals?

A goal is something you want to achieve in the future. In this section, you will look at different kinds of goals and read about a person with 127 goals.

1. Identify

Listen and read these captions. What are these students' goals?

Robert Thomas is a high school senior.

I plan to get a job next year. I'd like to work as a carpenter. I also hope to go to college part-time.

2. Interview

Pairwork. List the students' goals from Activity 1. Then ask a partner about them.

Do you want to . . . ?	Yes	No	Maybe
go to college after high school			✓
work as a computer programmer			
travel around the world			

Report your partner's YES answer to the class.

Example: *Min wants to go to college after high school.*

3. List

On your own. What are your goals? List several ideas.

I want to _____
I hope to _____
I'd like to _____
_____
_____
_____

4. Analyze

Classwork. The pictures on the next page give information about John Goddard's goals. What do you think his goals are?

Language Focus:

Asking For and Giving Information

Q: Do you want to go to college after high school?
A: Yes, I do. (No, I don't./Maybe./I'm not sure.)

My Life's List

When John Goddard was fifteen years old, he made a list of things that he wanted to do during his lifetime. By the time he finished, there were 127 goals on his list.

Some of Goddard's goals involved travel and exploration:
- *Explore the Amazon (a river in South America).*
- *Visit every country in the world.*

Other goals dealt with learning new things:
- *Play the flute and violin.*
- *Fly a plane.*
- *Type 50 words a minute.*
- *Make a parachute jump.*

Some of his goals were intellectually demanding:
- *Write a book.*
- *Compose music.*

Other goals were physically demanding:
- *Broad jump fifteen feet (4.6 meters).*
- *Climb the Matterhorn (a mountain in Switzerland).*
- *Ride an elephant, a camel, an ostrich, and a bucking bronco.*

John Goddard was serious about his list of goals. Over the next 50 years, he reached 108 of the goals on his list. And he is still working to reach the remaining 19 goals.

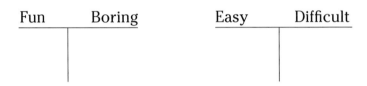

6. Classify

a. Pairwork. Classify John Goddard's goals. Use these categories or think of your own.

Dangerous	Not Dangerous
make a parachute jump	play the flute

Fun   Boring   Easy   Difficult

b. Share your work with the class.

7. Identify

a. Pairwork. Choose one of the goals on page 73. What should you do to reach this goal? Write your ideas.

Examples:

Goal:	What should you do to reach this goal?
Type 50 words a minute	Take a typing course
	Practice a lot

Goal:	What should you do to reach this goal?
Climb the Matterhorn	Get in good physical condition (Exercise a lot!)
	Save money to pay for the trip
	Learn about mountain climbing

b. Share your ideas with the class.

Language Focus:

Agreeing and Disagreeing

Agreeing
A: I think making a parachute jump is dangerous.
B: I agree. (So do I./I think so too.)

Disagreeing
A: I think writing a book is fun.
B: I disagree. (I don't think so./ I'm not sure about that.)

Language Focus:

Giving Advice

- You should take a typing course.
- You should practice a lot.

8. Write

a. On your own. Add to your list of goals. Think of goals for each of these categories. (Some goals may fit in more than one category.) Share your chart with a classmate.

Goals				
Travel	**Learning New Things**	**Intellectual**	**Physical**	**Personal**
visit Russia	learn to speak Russian	graduate from a university	become a good swimmer	make some new friends get married

b. Choose one of your goals. Tell what you are going to do to reach this goal.

Goal	**What are you going to do to reach this goal?**
Learn to speak Russian	*Practice speaking with a Russian person* *Take a course in Russian* *Study hard* *Listen to tapes* *Read books in Russian* *Memorize words*

> **Language Focus:**
>
> **Describing Future Plans**
>
> ■ I'm going to take a course in Russian.
> ■ I'm going to listen to language tapes.

c. Write about one of your goals. Tell what you are going to do to reach your goal.

One of my goals is to _____ .

To reach this goal, I am going to _____ .

I am also going to _____

and _____ .

Another thing I can do to reach my goal is to

_____ .

If I do all of these things, I might reach my goal.

Reaching your goals: A folktale

Stories about foolish people exist in many cultures. In Haiti, people tell stories about a foolish man named Bouki. In the story in this section, Bouki tries to reach a goal. Read to find out what happens.

1. Preview

a. Classwork. Use the pictures and captions on page 77 to make a K-W-L chart.

Answer these questions before you read the story.

Answer this question after you read the story.

Know	Want to know	Learned
What do you know about the story from the pictures?	What do you want to know?	What did you learn?
Bouki was in a city. Many people were reading newspapers.	Why was he in the city? Why were they reading newspapers?	

b. In the story on page 77, Bouki has a goal. What do you think his goal is? Make a prediction.

Bouki wants to _____

_____

_____

_____.

Bouki's Glasses

One day, Bouki was in the big city of Port-au-Prince. All around, he saw people reading newspapers. Now, there was one thing Bouki really wanted to do. More than anything, he wanted to read a newspaper. So after he sold his yams and coconuts, he went to a store that sold eyeglasses.

He tried on this pair of glasses and that pair. Finally, he found a pair that was just right. He bought the glasses and went outside. On the street he found a boy selling newspapers. He bought a newspaper and started home.

In the city, Bouki saw many people reading newspapers.

That evening, Bouki and his wife had dinner together. After dinner, Bouki took his chair and put it near the oil lamp. He sat down and put on his new glasses. He leaned back and opened his newspaper. He looked at the paper a long time. He turned the pages. He turned the paper upside down. He turned it around. He turned up the lamp so there would be more light. At last, he said: "They cheated me! These glasses are no good! I can't understand a word of this newspaper!"

After dinner, Bouki sat down to read the newspaper.

Bouki went to a store. He tried on many pairs of glasses.

He turned the newspaper upside down.

3. Share Ideas

a. Classwork. What is your reaction to the story? Discuss ideas with your classmates. Here are some questions to think about:

1. Did you like this story? Why or why not?
2. What was Bouki's goal?
3. What did he to do reach his goal?
4. Did he reach his goal? Why or why not?
5. This story is a folktale. Folktales often show how a culture thinks a person should behave. In this way, folktales try to teach a lesson. What lesson do you think this folktale is trying to teach?

b. Classwork. Think about Bouki's goal. What could he do to reach his goal? Where could he go for help? Who could help him? Think of several possibilities.

Language Focus:

Suggesting Possibilities

- He could go to school.
- He could _____ .

4. Use Context

a. On your own. Read these sentences from the story. Choose a word to complete each sentence.

comfortable/uncomfortable

1. Finally Bouki found a pair of glasses that were _____ . He bought them and went outside.

turned off/turned up

2. Bouki _____ the lamp so there would be more light.

very good/very bad

3. "These glasses are _____ ," Bouki said. "I can't understand a word of this newspaper!"

b. Pairwork. Compare sentences. Then answer these questions:

1. What words and ideas in the sentences helped you to choose a word?
2. Find the sentences above in the story on page 77. What words did the writer choose? Use context to guess the meaning of these words.

Study Strategy:

Using Context

Use the words and ideas in the sentences before and after a new word to guess its meaning.

Make a Story Map

a. Pairwork. What happened in the story? Make a story
   map of *Bouki's Glasses.*

Story Title: _____

> **Setting:**
> (Where?)

Characters: _____   _____
(Who?)   _____   _____

> **Initial Event:**
> (What happens first?)
> *Bouki saw people reading newspapers.*

Goal Setting: _____
(What is the main character's goal?)

> **Attempt to Reach Goal:**
> (What does the main character do to reach
> the goal?)

Outcome: _____
(What happens in the end?)

b. Compare story maps with another pair.

> **Study Strategy:**
>
> **Making a Story Map**
>
> A story map is a
> chart that shows
> the main elements
> of a story. Making a
> story map helps
> you understand a
> story.

a. Pairwork. Here are some things Bouki did in the story. Add three more things to the timeline.

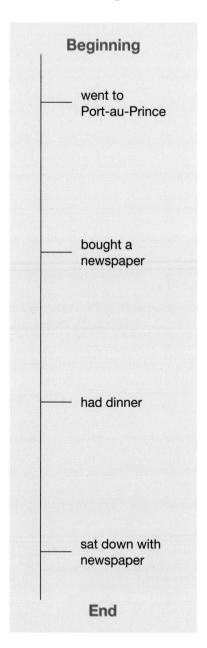

Beginning

went to Port-au-Prince

bought a newspaper

had dinner

sat down with newspaper

End

b. Use your timeline to retell the story.

7. Write a Summary

a. On your own. Write a summary of the story *Bouki's Glasses.*

> Bouki
>
> wanted _to read a newspaper._
>
> So, _____
>
> but _____
>
> In the end, _____

b. Compare summaries with a partner.

8. Extend

Groupwork. Read the last paragraph of the story again. In writing, tell what Bouki did next. Share your writing with the class.

Reaching your goals: A song

It may seem difficult to reach some of your goals. You might want to give up, or stop trying. Instead of giving up, follow the advice in the song "You Can Get It If You Really Want."

1. **Quickwrite**

a. On your own. Choose a goal from your list on page 75. Quickwrite about this goal for five minutes. Here are some questions you might think about:

- Why is this goal important to you?
- Will this goal be difficult to reach? Why or why not?
- What problems might you have?

b. Tell a partner about your goal.

2. **Match**

a. Groupwork. What advice would you give to these students? Write your ideas. Then share your group's ideas with the class.

"I tried to get good grades this year, but I didn't."

"I practice playing the guitar every day, but I still can't play very well."

"I want to study Arabic but it's very difficult. Maybe I should study something easier."

Study Strategy:

Quickwriting

Quickwriting is a good way to collect ideas. When you quickwrite, try to write without stopping.

b. Choose one of these proverbs to give advice to each of the students above.

Proverbs

- If you don't succeed at first, try again. (Don't stop trying.)
- The harder the battle, the sweeter the victory. (The more difficult something is to do, the better you will feel when you do it.)
- Rome was not built in a day. (Be patient. It takes time to reach your goals.)

3. **Shared Reading**

Read this song aloud with your classmates.

> **You Can Get It If You Really Want**
>
> (*chorus*)
> **You can get it if you really want (3x)**
> **But you must try, try, and try**
> **Try and try**
> **Till you succeed at last**
>
> Persecution you must bear
> Win or lose you got to get your share
> Got your mind set on a dream
> You can get it tho' hard it may seem
>
> Rome was not built in a day
> Opposition will come your way
> But the harder the battle you see
> It's the sweeter the victory
>
> —*Jimmy Cliff*

Rome

JIMMY CLIFF

Jimmy Cliff, born James Chambers in Jamaica in 1948, is one of the most well-known reggae performers. He performed at the New York World's Fair in 1964, then went to England and Brazil to record his music. After a brief movie career, Jimmy studied Islam in Africa. He continued recording through the '80's, when Bruce Springsteen recorded his version of Cliff's "Trapped." This new attention to Cliff earned him a role in the movie *Club Paradise* with Robin Williams.

4. Share Ideas

Classwork. What's your reaction to the song? Share ideas with your classmates. Here are some questions to think about:

a. What does the song mean to you?

b. Read the title of the song. What do you think the word *it* means?

c. Use the ideas in the song to give some advice to Bouki, the main character in the story on page 77.

d. The song "You Can Get It If You Really Want" is a reggae song. Have you ever heard any reggae music? What was it like?

5. Write

a. On your own. Complete this sentence in different ways.

You can _____ *if you* _____ .

Examples:

You can __go to college__ if you __study hard__ .

You can __earn some money__ if you __get a job__ .

b. Choose one of your sentences. Write it in large letters on a piece of paper.

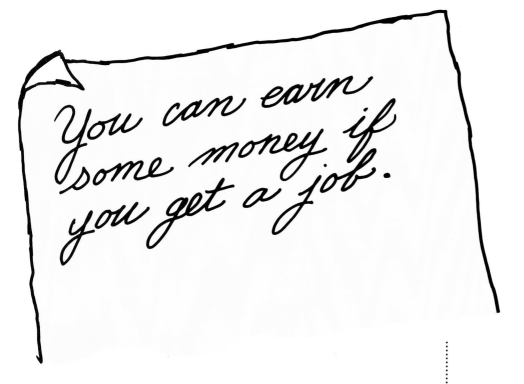

You can earn some money if you get a job.

c. Groupwork. Get together in groups of six or more. Follow these instructions:

- One student collects your group's papers.
- Together, read all of the sentences aloud.
- Change the order of the papers.
- Read the sentences aloud again.
- Experiment with the order of sentences.
- Choose the order that sounds best. Together, read the lines aloud as a poem. If you want, add a chorus.
- Read your poem to the class.

Career goals identify the type of work you want to do. In this section, you will read about people in different jobs and think about your own career goals.

1. Match

Classwork. Match these careers with the job descriptions below.

Transportation Planner

Computer Specialist

Sports Reporter

Jewelry Designer

Career	Job Description (What do you do in your job?)
Computer Specialist	"I teach people how to use their equipment. I also fix equipment."
	"I make things with my hands."
	"I interview people and write about special events."
	"I do research and write a lot of reports."

2. **Jigsaw**

Groupwork. Read one of the questionnaires below or listen to the interview. Take notes in a chart.

Career: _____

Activities	Likes	Dislikes	Skills/Training	How to Prepare

Four people answered questions about their careers. Their answers are on these questionnaires.

Questionnaire #1: A Transportation Planner

1. **What is your job?**

   I work as a Transportation Planner.

2. **What do you do in your job?**

   I do a lot of research. I study the transportation needs of people—where they need to go and how. I use this information to predict where a town or city will need new roads, bus lines, etc. I also go to a lot of meetings to collect information. And I write a lot of reports, using a computer.

3. **What do you like and dislike about your job?**

   I like looking for ways to solve problems. I spend a lot of time writing and I like that. I also like working in an office and getting a good salary. Sometimes I have to work outdoors in cold weather (counting cars) and I don't like that.

4. **What kinds of skills and training do you need?**

   You should be able to think about all sides of a problem. You should also be able to write clearly.

   To get a job as a Transportation Planner, you should get a college degree.

5. **What can students do to prepare for this career?**

   They should study mathematics, science, and English. And learning to write clearly is important.

Questionnaire #2: Computer Specialist

1. **What is your job?**

   I'm a Computer Specialist.

2. **What do you do in your job?**

   I spend a lot of time fixing computers and helping people. I teach them how to use their computers. Computers are always changing, so I have to read a lot of technical books and magazines.

3. **What do you like and dislike about your job?**

   I'm always learning something new—I like that. I also enjoy working with people. But sometimes I have too much work and I don't like that.

4. **What kinds of skills and training do you need?**

   It's helpful to have a degree in Computer Science. You should also be able to communicate well with people.

5. **What can students do to prepare for this career?**

   Take computer classes in high school. Use computers whenever possible. Get a college education.

Questionnaire #3: Sports Reporter

1. **What is your job?**

   I write about sports for a newspaper.

2. **What do you do in your job?**

   I go to sports games and write about them. I interview athletes and coaches. I spend a lot of time on the telephone talking to people and getting information. I also do a lot of typing.

3. **What do you like and dislike about your job?**

   I like playing with words.

   I have to do lots of different things. Every day is different. I like that.

   I don't like spending so much time on the phone.

   Sometimes I have to work on the weekends and I don't like that.

4. **What kinds of skills and training do you need?**

   You need good communication skills. A knowledge of sports helps, too. But most of all, you should be curious and observant.

5. **What can students do to prepare for this career?**

   Read as many books as you can. Learn to type. Keep a diary. Writing is a skill that you can learn.

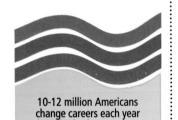

10-12 million Americans change careers each year (1986). That's 10 percent of the people who work.

Questionnaire #4: Jewelry Designer

1. **What is your job?**

   I'm a jewelry designer.

2. **What do you do in your job?**

   I spend a lot of time drawing my ideas for a piece of jewelry. Then I work with special tools and materials to make jewelry. I also have to sell my work and keep records of my sales and expenses.

3. **What do you like and dislike about your job?**

   I like almost everything about my job. I love making beautiful things. I like working by myself—I'm my own boss. I don't like keeping records, but it's an important part of the job.

4. **What kinds of skills and training do you need?**

   First of all, you need to be creative. You also need to study art and learn to use special tools and materials. And you have to be good with your hands.

5. **What can students do to prepare for this career?**

   Take art, math, and science courses. Draw a lot. Learn to use a computer.

3. **Share Information**

Groupwork. Get together with a new group of students. Find out about the three other careers. Take notes in a chart.

Career: _____

Activities	Likes	Dislikes	Skills/Training	How to Prepare

4. Apply

a. On your own. Match these students' interests and abilities with a career. Use the information in your charts.

Careers: Transportation Planner, Computer Specialist, Sports Reporter, Jewelry Designer

Interests and Abilities	**Career Suggestions**
1. "I enjoy writing, but I don't want to work in an office."	*Sports Reporter*
2. "I like writing and working with numbers. My favorite school subjects are math and English."	_____
3. "I like making things with my hands. I'd like to have my own business."	_____
4. "I'm good at fixing things, but I also like working with people. I don't want to sit at a desk all day."	_____

In 1991, 21.4% of Americans 25 years and older ahd completed four years of college or more.

b. Compare ideas with a partner.

c. Can you think of other careers for these people? Share your ideas with the class.

5. ▷ **Self-evaluate**

a. On your own. Which career might be good for you? Complete these checklists to find out.

Transportation Planner			
Are you interested in _____ ?	**Very interested (2 points each)**	**A little interested (1 point each)**	**Not interested at all (0 points each)**
doing research	✓	—	—
going to meetings	—	✓	—
writing reports	—	✓	—
using a computer	—	✓	—
working in an office	—	—	✓

SUBTOTAL: __1__ × 2 = __2__   __3__ × 1 = __3__   __1__ × 0 = __0__

TOTAL: 2 + 3 + 0 = 5

Computer Specialist			
Are you interested in _____ ?	**Very interested (2 points each)**	**A little interested (1 point each)**	**Not interested at all (0 points each)**
fixing things	—	—	—
helping people	—	—	—
teaching	—	—	—
reading technical information	—	—	—
using a computer	—	—	—

SUBTOTAL: __ × 2 = __   __ × 1 = __   __ × 0 = __

TOTAL: __ + __ + __ = __

Sports Reporter			
Are you interested in _____ ?	Very interested (2 points each)	A little interested (1 point each)	Not interested at all (0 points each)
going to sports games	—	—	—
interviewing people	—	—	—
talking on the telephone	—	—	—
working unusual hours	—	—	—
using a computer	—	—	—

SUBTOTAL: __ × 2 = __   __ × 1 = __   __ × 0 = __

TOTAL: __ + __ + __ = __

Jewelry Designer			
Are you interested in _____ ?	Very interested (2 points each)	A little interested (1 point each)	Not interested at all (0 points each)
working with your hands	—	—	—
drawing pictures	—	—	—
selling things	—	—	—
keeping business records	—	—	—
working by yourself	—	—	—

SUBTOTAL: __ × 2 = __   __ × 1 = __   __ × 0 = __

TOTAL: __ + __ + __ = __

b. Look at your total for each checklist. Which career has the highest number? Does this surprise you? Why or why not?

6. Collect Information

Classwork. Give a copy of this questionnaire to people in different careers. Use their answers to make a self-evaluation checklist.

1. What is your job?

2. What do you do in your job?

3. What do you like and dislike about your job?

4. What kind of skills and training do you need?

5. What can students do to prepare for this career?

Goals of the U.S. government

Like individuals, governments have goals. In this section, you will read about the goals of the U.S. government and what it does to reach these goals.

1. List

a. Groupwork. There are more than 160 countries in the world. Each of these countries has a government. Why? List your ideas.

Why do countries have governments?

_____

_____

_____

_____

b. Share your group's ideas with the class.

2. Match

Classwork. What can a government do to reach these goals? Match each picture with a goal.

GOALS

- defend the country from attack
- provide for the well-being (good living and working conditions) of people
- provide ways to settle disputes, or disagreements

Provide courts

Provide schools

Provide a military force

Build roads

 Speculate

a. Groupwork. Think about the questions in the chart below. Guess answers to the questions and write them in the chart.

	My Guess	**Text Information**
How much money does the U.S. government spend each year?		
How many people work for the U.S. government?		
What are the goals of the U.S. government?		

b. Read or listen to the passage on pages 96–99. Look for answers to the questions above and write them in the chart.

What are the goals of the U.S. government?

The U.S. government spends more than 1,000,000,000,000 (one trillion) dollars every year. It employs more than 3,117,000 people. It represents more than two hundred million people.

Why does the government spend so much money and employ so many people? To answer this question, just think about what the government has to do— what its goals are.

The goals of the U.S. government are stated in the Preamble (introduction) to the U.S. Constitution. The Constitution is a set of laws that define what the government can do. It also tells how the government should do these things. These laws were written more than 200 years ago when the United States became an independent country. The Preamble states that the goals of the government are to:

1. make sure all people are treated equally

2. promote peace within the United States

3. defend the country against attack

4. provide for the well-being of all people

5. protect our freedoms and make certain that our children have the same freedoms

The U.S. Constitution.

And what does the U.S. government do to reach these goals? Here are a few examples:

- The U.S. government maintains a military force to defend the country. There are 2.1 million men and women in the U.S. Army, Navy, Marine Corps, and Air Force.

- It builds superhighways.

- It enforces laws that forbid discrimination, or unequal treatment, in public places such as restaurants and hotels.

- It provides loans for students who want to go to college. About five million students receive these loans each year.

- It provides food stamps to about 26 million people. People can use food stamps to buy food.

- It protects the right of people to protest, or express their disagreement with a law. If people think a law is unfair, they can express their disagreement peacefully.

- It provides a system of courts to settle disputes fairly and peacefully.

- It supports research into the causes and cures of disease.

- It makes sure that food is safe to eat.

5. Match

a. Groupwork. Match the activities of the U.S. government with one or more of its goals.

1. to make sure all people are treated equally
2. to promote peace
3. to defend the country
4. to provide for the well-being of all people
5. to protect our freedoms

Activities of the U.S. Government	to make sure all people are treated equally	to promote peace	to defend the country	to provide for the well-being of all people	to protect our freedoms
The U.S. government maintains a military force.			✓		✓
It provides loans for college students.					
It provides food stamps.					
It provides a system of courts.					
It enforces laws that forbid discrimination.					
It makes sure food is safe to eat.					

b. On your own. Use your chart to complete these sentences.

1. One way the government promotes peace within the United States is by _providing a system of courts_ .

2. One way the government defends the country is by

_____

_____ .

3. One way the government provides for the well-being of people is by _____

_____.

4. One way the government makes sure people are treated equally is by _____

_____.

5. One way the government protects our freedoms is by

_____

_____.

6. List

a. Groupwork. One of the government's goals is to provide for the well-being of all people. What do you need for your well-being (to live a safe, healthy, and good life)? List your ideas.

_____*a job*_____

_____*a place to live*_____

_____

_____

b. What can you do to provide for your own well-being? List your ideas.

_____

_____

_____

c. What do you think the government should do to provide for the well-being of all people? List your ideas.

_____

_____

_____

d. Share your group's ideas with the class.

The U.S. Government spends hundreds of billions of dollars each year to maintain its armed forces.

Activity Menu

Choose one of the following activities to do.

1. Make a Poster
Make a poster telling about one of your goals. Use pictures and words to explain what you are going to do to reach this goal. Choose a place in the classroom to display your poster.

2. Collect Pictures
Collect pictures of people in different occupations. Label the pictures and use them to make a wall display of career information.

3. Make a Career Alphabet
Write the letters of the alphabet in a vertical list. Identify a career that begins with each letter of the alphabet. Tell what people in these careers do.

A Architect—designs buildings
B Botanist—studies plants

4. Make a Plan
Work with a group of students. Together, choose a goal that you can reach in one week. Together, decide what you need to do to reach this goal. Decide what each person in your group will do. At the end of the week, tell the class what your group did. Include answers to these questions in your report to the class.

- What was your goal?
- Did you reach your goal?
- What did you learn from doing this project?
- What skills did you use to do your project?

5. Write a Story That Teaches a Lesson
Use a story map like the one on page 79 to write a new story. First, organize your ideas by completing the story map. Then use the map to write the story. Read your story to someone in your class.

6. Explore a Career

Look for books about careers in your school library or career center. Read about a career that interests you. Collect information in a chart like this:

Job Description	Salary	Skills and Training Needed

Use the chart to tell your classmates about this career.

7. Listen and Take Notes

Invite your school guidance counselor or career center director to speak to your class about careers. Before this person comes to your class, prepare a list of questions to ask. Take notes on the speaker's answers to your questions.

8. Investigate an Organization

Choose an organization that interests you. Read or talk to people about the organization. Find out about the organization's goals. Make a list of the goals and present them to your classmates.

Some suggested organizations:
- a school club
- a school sports teams
- a town or city organization

9. Collect Data

Go to the library. Find information about the number of people in different careers. Use the data to make a graph. Write about your findings.

Read on...

David Klein

My parents' plans for me include
College,
Medical School,
Internship,
Residency,
Private practice.
They do not include Jennie,
Jennie, who makes me think of
Walks along the shore,
Quick kisses in the movies,
Frisbee-tossing in the park.
"You'll meet the right type of girl,"
   my mother says,
Not making the least attempt to be subtle.
"Somebody with a similar background,"
   my father says,
Not making the least attempt to be understanding.
The thought of Chinese-Jewish grandchildren
Terrifies them.
If I am going to be a doctor
And hold life and death in my hands,
Why can't I take charge of my own life
And hold the hand
Of the girl I love?

by Mel Glenn

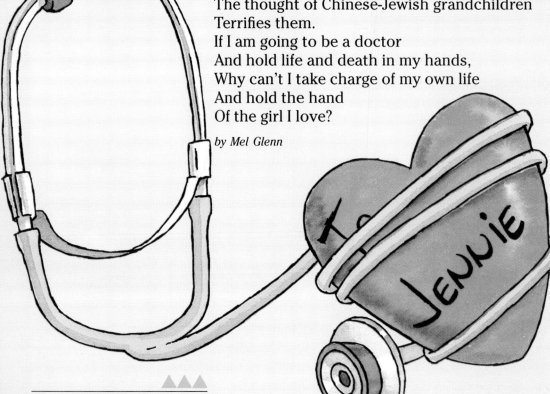

Homero E. Acevedo II

Homero E. Acevedo II is an executive with the American Telephone and Telegraph Company (AT&T). Mr. Acevedo has used his good education and his ability to communicate well in English and Spanish to become one of the youngest managers of the AT&T National Bilingual Center in San Antonio, Texas. There are lots of things we can learn from Mr. Acevedo.

Mr. Acevedo is very close to his family. Born in 1961, he is the youngest child. His family includes his late father, Homero, Sr., his mother, Maria, his two sisters, Annette and Angelique, and his twin brothers, Hugo and Hector.

When Mr. Acevedo was young, he was never lonesome with his brothers and sisters around. He especially remembers going down the stairs Christmas morning when his father made home movies and blinded him with bright floodlights.

His father and mother always encouraged him to get a good education, share with others, love others, work hard, and be all that he could be. They were also a good example for him. His parents were and still are his heroes. Some day, he hopes to have a beautiful family of his own.

Mr. Acevedo's parents gave him advice about how to handle teasing and prejudice. His father told him that if someone thought there was something wrong with him because he was Hispanic, then that person must not have been educated very well and should be ignored. So, that is exactly what he has done. He is proud of who he is.

Mr. Acevedo's dad taught him what goals are and helped him achieve some. One of his goals was to become an outstanding athlete. He did, and his favorite sports were soccer, baseball, and basketball. At one point, he played semiprofessional soccer. He loves Chicago teams, especially the Bears, Bulls, Cubs, and Blackhawks.

Although sports are an important part of Mr. Acevedo's life, they never became his main goal.

The most important goal was to get a good education. Mr. Acevedo realized that a good education would open many doors for him in the future. In high school, he studied hard and made excellent grades. He then graduated from the University of Denver. While in college, he had a chance to study in Spain. By being one of the top academic students, he got to meet the king of Spain, Juan Carlos.

Mr. Acevedo knew that he needed to be ready to move to different parts of the country to advance in his career. He moved to New Jersey for training. He was in charge of testing a new billing system and a new computer system that would take care of eighty million residential customer accounts. This was a great responsibility.

After six months of testing the computer system, he was moved to San Antonio, Texas. There he is an operations manager in charge of the International Communications Service Center. Many office managers report to him. There are about 175 people in his department. He makes sure that everything runs smoothly.

Mr. Acevedo is able to communicate with people very well. He can speak and write fluent English and Spanish. He feels very lucky to know two languages and believes it has helped him be a successful executive. He says, "Anyone can be a success if they are secure with themselves, ready to move, and an achiever."

▼A changing population

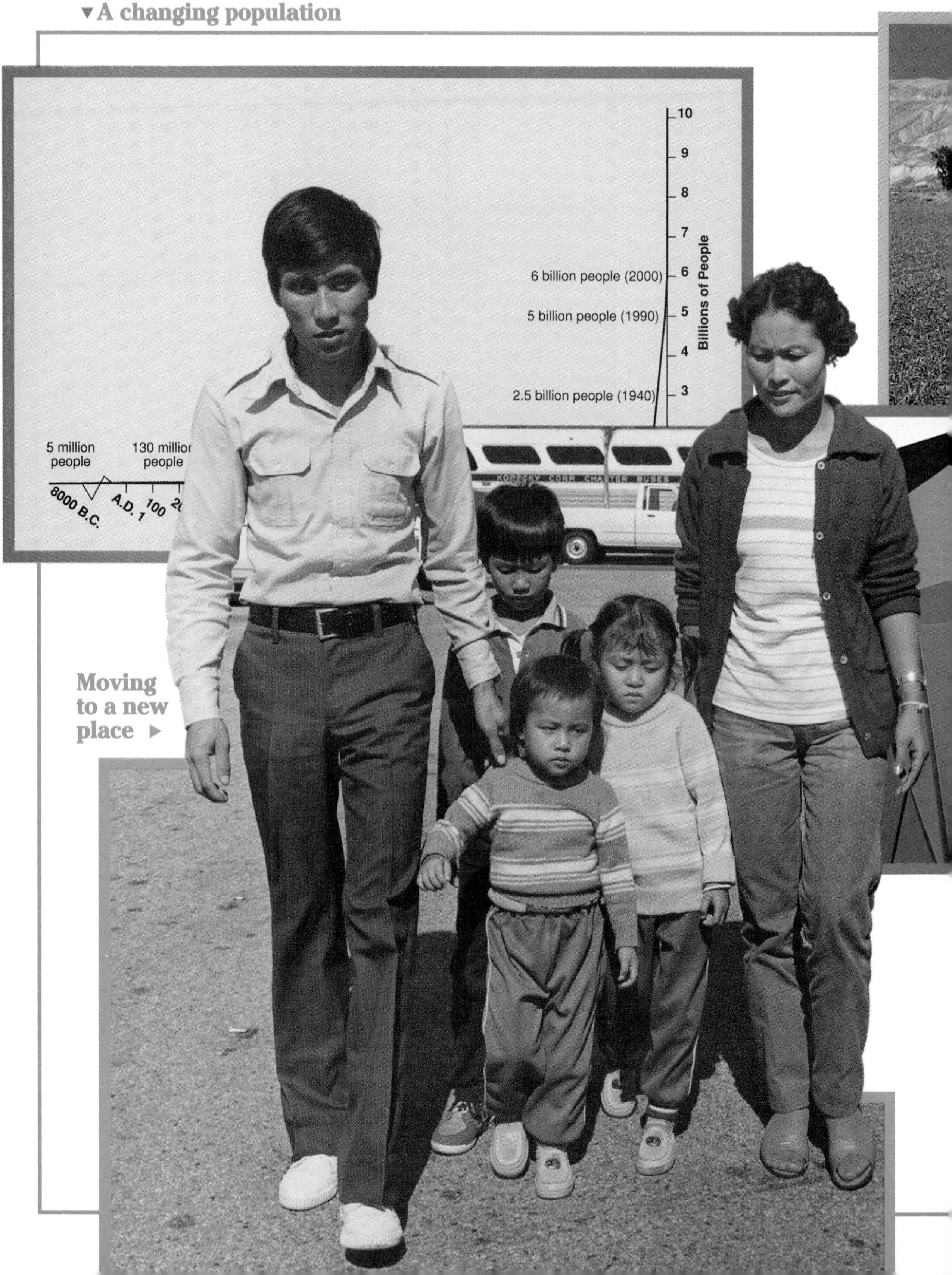
10
9
8
7
6 billion people (2000)
6
5 billion people (1990)
5
4
2.5 billion people (1940)
3
Billions of People
5 million people
130 million people
8000 B.C.
A.D. 1
100
KOPECKY CORR CHARTER BUSES

Moving to a new place ▶

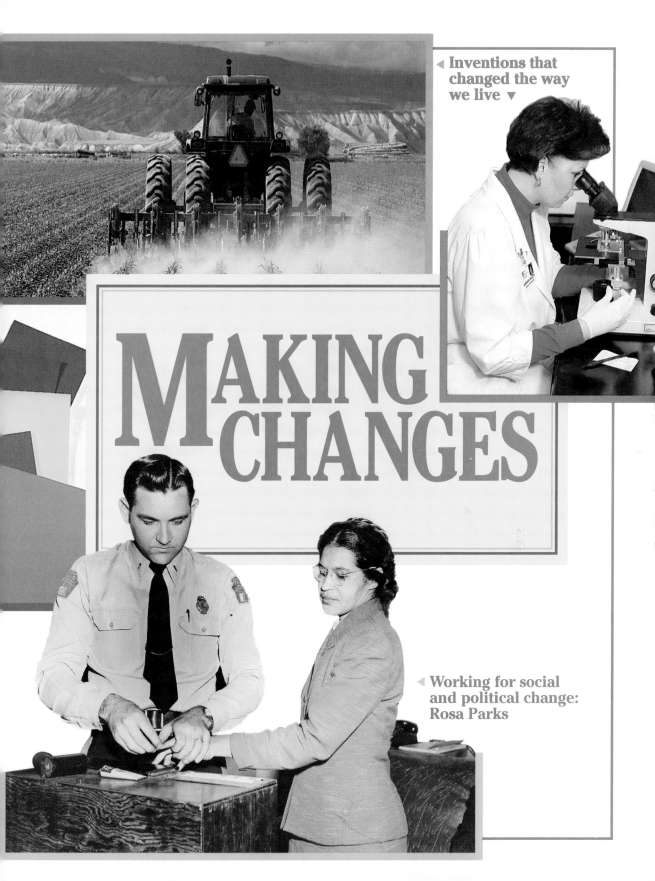

◀ Inventions that
changed the way
we live ▼

MAKING
CHANGES

◀ Working for social
and political change:
Rosa Parks

Moving to a new place:
An autobiographical account

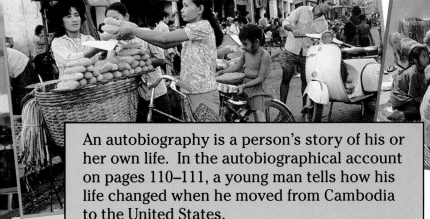

An autobiography is a person's story of his or her own life. In the autobiographical account on pages 110–111, a young man tells how his life changed when he moved from Cambodia to the United States.

1. Identify

a. Classwork. Think about your first days in the United States. What was new or different for you? Share ideas with your classmates.

Example: *Everyone spoke English.*
It was very rainy.

b. Classwork. Ponn Pet moved to the United States from Cambodia. What do you think was new or different for him in the United States? List your ideas on the board.

Things that were different in the United States

the food
_____
_____

2. Take Notes in a Chart

On your own. As you read the story below, take notes in a chart.

Changes in Ponn Pet's Life

	In Cambodia	In the United States	Same or Different?
Climate	*warm*	*cold*	*different*
People			
Food			
Language			
Customs			

3. Shared Reading

An Immigrant in the United States

I am a Cambodian immigrant refugee living in the United States. My family and I left Cambodia because of the war in the country where I was born. I can't believe that we are free in this country.

I was eight years old when I first saw different colored people. How strange, scary, and frightening to see white and black colored people, red and brown and yellow hair, blue, green, and brown eyes. I thought they had costumes on. My eyes had only seen brown-skinned people with black hair. The only pictures in books I had ever seen in my country were of Cambodian people who are of the brown race.

Study Strategy:

Taking Notes in a Chart

Taking notes in a chart will help you to organize information. This helps you remember it.

Everything was different here. The climate was so cold, and when I saw something white on the ground, I thought somebody went up in an airplane and dropped lots and lots of tiny pieces of paper down on the ground. It was the first time I saw snow. When I went to school, I couldn't speak English and the teacher didn't speak Khmer. I couldn't understand what to do. It was very difficult. Eating in the cafeteria at the beginning was so different. I had never seen or tasted milk and never eaten cheese or butter. I had never used a fork or a knife. There were about five other Cambodian kids in my room who had been in America longer, so they showed me how to use a fork and a knife. At first, I didn't like the foods—cheese, salad, pizza, and milk—so I threw them away. The foods I hated are some of my favorite foods now, like pizza, cheese, and milk.

American kids showed me how to play American sports and we became friends. Today, I feel very happy to be in America, a free country. The color of people doesn't scare me anymore. I think how silly it was to be afraid. Everyone is the same inside with the same feelings.

—*Ponn Pet*

 4. **Compare and Contrast**

a. Groupwork. Compare charts from Activity 2.

b. Groupwork. Take turns writing a sentence about Ponn Pet's life in Cambodia and in the United States. Use your chart for ideas.

> Ponn Pet used to live in a warm climate, but now he lives in a cold climate.
> He used to speak Khmer at school, but now he speaks English.

c. Share your group's sentences with the class.

5. Write

a. On your own. Tell about life in your native country and in the United States. List your ideas in a chart.

	In My Native Country	In the United States	Same or Different?
Climate			
People			
Food			
Language			
Customs			

b. Pairwork. Tell a partner about the ideas in your chart.

c. Write about the changes in your life. Use your chart for ideas.

Paragraph 1
Introduction

> Where are you from? Why did you move here?

Paragraph 2

> What was new or different for you here?

Paragraph 3
Conclusion

> How do you feel about the changes in your life?

d. Share your writing with a classmate.

Inventions that changed the way we live

The way we live today is different from the way our grandparents and great-grandparents lived. In this section, you will read about some of the inventions that have made these changes possible.

1. Identify

a. Classwork. What do we use these things for? Share ideas with your classmates.

These inventions changed the way people live.

Language Focus:

Identifying Purpose

Q: What do we use a sewing machine for?
A: To make clothes.

Q: What do we use a telephone for?
A: To talk to people far away.

Air Conditioner (1911)

Personal Computer (1981)

Telephone (1876)

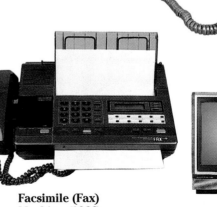

Facsimile (Fax) Machine (1988)

Television (1930)

Sewing Machine (1846)

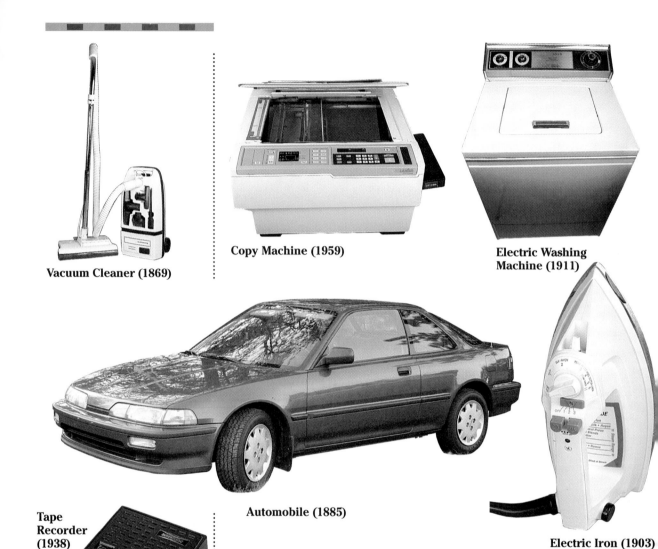

Vacuum Cleaner (1869)

Copy Machine (1959)

Electric Washing Machine (1911)

Automobile (1885)

Electric Iron (1903)

Tape Recorder (1938)

Pocket Calculator (1971)

b. Pairwork. Answer the questions in a chart. Then share answers with your classmates.

Invention	What do you use it for?	What did people use before?
sewing machine	*to make clothes*	*their hands*
telephone	*to talk to people at a distance*	
vacuum cleaner		
automobile		

 2. **Compare**

Pairwork. Take turns telling about life in the past and today. Use your chart from Activity 1 for ideas.

Student A: People used to _make clothes by hand_ .
Student B: Today they _use sewing machines_ .

Student B: People used to _travel by horse_ .
Student A: Today they _travel by car_ .

3. **Evaluate**

a. Pairwork. Choose one invention. List the advantages and disadvantages of this invention.

Invention: _washing machine_

Advantages	**Disadvantages**
+	–
You can wash clothes quickly.	_It uses a lot of water._
You can save a lot of time.	

b. Share your ideas with the class. Together, answer this question:

Do the advantages outweigh the disadvantages? (Are the advantages more important than the disadvantages?)

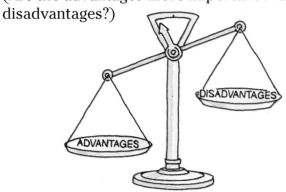

Thomas Edison invented 1,093 things. Among his inventions are the phonograph, the light bulb, and the motion picture projector.

4. Match

Classwork. Match the photographs and the years.

1850   1910   1950   1990

What helps you to date the photographs?

5. Make a K-W-L Chart

a. Groupwork. Choose one of these inventions. Write your ideas about this invention in a K-W-L chart.

Plow

Paper

Microscope

Answer these questions before you read the passage.

Answer this question after you read the passage.

Invention: _Paper_

Know	Want to Know	Learned
What do you know about this invention?	What do you want to find out?	What did you learn?
Paper is made from trees.	*Who invented paper?*	

Study Strategy:

Making a K-W-L Chart

Making a K-W-L chart is a good way to get ready to read.

b. Share your chart with the class.

The first paper was made from the bark of trees and old rags.

Before paper was invented, people carved information on stone.

Thousands of years ago, people wrote on wet clay. Then they baked the clay tablets until hard.

Read or listen to the section about your group's invention and complete your K-W-L chart.

Paper

Before paper was invented, people wrote on materials such as stone, clay tablets, and parchment. But none of these writing surfaces worked very well. Stone was difficult to carve. Clay tablets were heavy to carry around, and parchment was expensive to make. Around A.D. 105 a Chinese man by the name of Ts'ai Lun invented a much better writing surface—paper. It is believed that Ts'ai Lun used the bark of trees and old rags to make paper. His paper was light, easy to write on, and cheap to make. The Chinese kept the invention of paper a secret for several hundred years. But eventually, people in other parts of the world learned the art of paper making.

Paper was a very important invention because it provided a way to record information easily and cheaply. With paper, people could more easily make copies of written information. This made it possible to communicate ideas and information to a larger number of people.

Today, there are more than 7,000 different kinds of paper. Much of this paper is used for written communication, but we also use it to make paper products like cardboard boxes and paper plates.

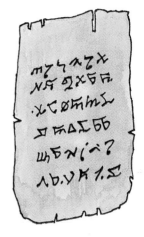

Parchment was made from the skin of animals.

The Plow

Thousands of years ago people discovered that plants grow better in soil that has been loosened. For a long time, farmers used sharp sticks, rocks, and other objects to loosen the soil. Then about 8,000 years ago, someone in the Middle East came up with the idea for a plow. These early plows were simple forked sticks pulled by a person. About a thousand years later, people began using oxen to pull simple plows. Today, many farmers use tractors to pull huge plows.

The plow was a very important invention because it allowed people to farm more land and grow more food. Because farmers could grow more food, fewer people died of starvation.

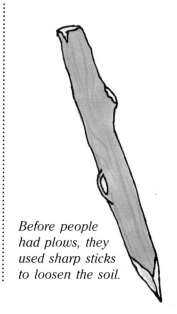

Before people had plows, they used sharp sticks to loosen the soil.

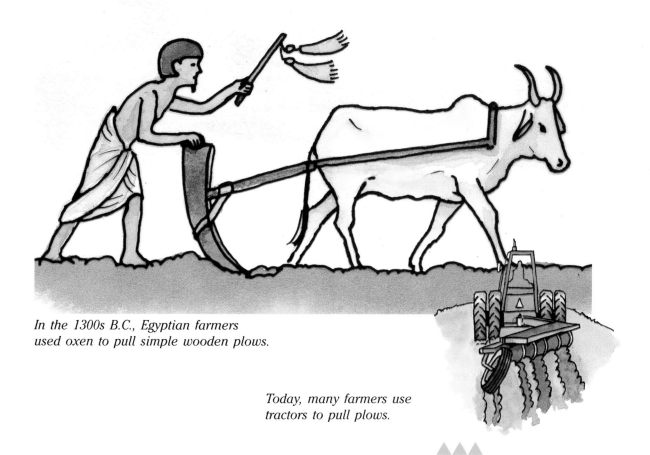

In the 1300s B.C., Egyptian farmers used oxen to pull simple wooden plows.

Today, many farmers use tractors to pull plows.

The Microscope

A microscope magnifies things, or makes them look larger. The simplest kind of microscope is a magnifying glass, which has one convex lens.

More than a thousand years ago, people used water-filled glass globes and rock crystals as magnifying glasses. Then in the 1300s, people learned how to make more powerful lenses. They used these lenses to make eyeglasses. In the 1600s, Anton van Leeuwenhoek, a Dutch merchant, found a way to make an even better lens. His lens could magnify things more than 200 times their natural size. In 1674, Leeuwenhoek, using a single lens microscope, was the first person to observe bacteria (very small organisms).

The invention of the microscope made it possible for scientists to learn how certain bacteria cause disease and infection. With this knowledge, scientists were able to look for ways to stop the spread of disease. Millions and millions of lives were saved because of the microscope.

A magnifying glass makes objects look larger.

A convex lens is thicker in the middle than at the edges. It can make objects look larger.

You can observe bacteria with a microscope.

More than a thousand years ago, people used water-filled globes and rock crystals to magnify objects.

7. Test Your Knowledge

Groupwork. Take turns asking and answering questions about your group's invention.

Example: *Q: What is a plow used for?*
               A: To loosen the soil.

8. Interview

Groupwork. Get together in new groups. Ask questions about the other inventions. Write your classmates' answers in a chart.

> ### *Language Focus:*
> #### *Asking "Wh" Questions*
>
> - What is _____ used for?
> - What did people use before _____ was invented?
> - Who invented _____ ?
> - When was _____ invented?
> - Why was the invention of the _____ important?

Invention	Used For?	Use Before?	Who?	When?	Why important?
Paper Plow Microscope					

9. Ask Questions

Groupwork. Follow these instructions to play a game:

- One person reads an answer from the chart in Activity 8.
- Without looking at the chart, your teammates match the answer with a question.

Example:

Answer	Question
Ts'ai Lun	*Who invented paper?*
at least 6,000 years ago	*When was the plow invented?*

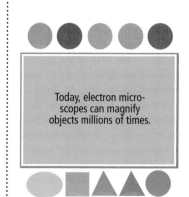

Today, electron microscopes can magnify objects millions of times.

◆ 10. Analyze

Classwork. What did these inventions make it possible for people to do? Share ideas with your classmates.

Language Focus:

Identifying Cause and Effect

■ The invention of paper made it possible to record information easily.

■ The invention of the plow made it possible to grow more food.

CAUSE	EFFECT
The invention of paper	*made it possible to record information easily*
The invention of the plow	
The invention of the microscope	

◆ 11. Evaluate

a. Groupwork. What were the five most important inventions of all time? List your ideas.

b. Groupwork. Why were these inventions important? List your ideas.

CAUSE	EFFECT
The invention of the *television*	*made it possible to get news quickly*
The invention of _____	
The invention of _____	

c. Groupwork. Together, choose the most important invention on your list. Tell why you think it was the most important invention. Report your ideas to the class.

A changing population

The population of the earth is changing rapidly. You will find out why in this section.

 1. **Solve a Word Problem**

a. Pairwork. Read this word problem and answer the questions.

Each day, about 400,000 babies are born around the world. On the same day, about 140,000 people die.

- How many more people are there in the world today than there were yesterday?
- How many more people will there be in a week? In 10 years?
- How is the world's population changing? Is it increasing, decreasing, or staying the same?

b. Get together with another pair. Tell how you solved the word problem.

Groupwork. Study the graph and answer the question below.

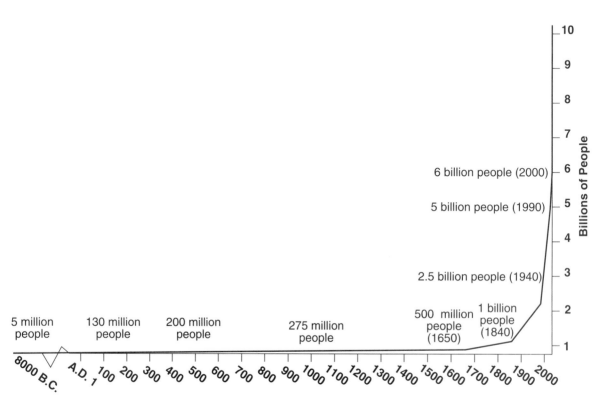

This line graph shows how the earth's population has changed. For thousands of years, the population increased very slowly. Since the mid-1800s, however, the earth's population has increased rapidly.

Why do you think the earth's population began to increase rapidly in the mid-1800s?

Study Strategy:

Reading a Line Graph

A line graph shows how something changes over time.

Guesses	Text Information
_____	_____
_____	_____
_____	_____

3. Shared Reading

a. Read to check your guesses from Activity 2.

My, How We've Grown

Why has the world's population grown so fast in the last 150 years? Beginning in the 1800s, many aspects of human life changed. Farms grew in size and number. New farming methods and better seeds increased annual harvests. People had more food to eat, and countries began buying and selling goods throughout the world. With the invention of new machines, people moved these goods—and themselves—quickly, first in steamships, then in trains, cars, and airplanes.

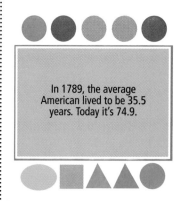

In 1789, the average American lived to be 35.5 years. Today it's 74.9.

After farming methods and transportation improved, cheap food became available to more people. Before these discoveries, famines—severe shortages of food—regularly caused widespread starvation. Famine is now a rare event in most parts of the world.

In addition to inventing ways to grow more food, scientists also discovered what caused some deadly diseases and infections. These scientists found out that certain bacteria (very tiny organisms) make us sick when they enter and grow in our bodies. After the invention of the microscope, scientists could see these tiny life forms and could learn how they caused sickness.

This important breakthrough helped to stop the spread of illnesses that pass rapidly from person to person through a population. These widespread diseases, known as epidemics, included malaria, influenza, and yellow fever.

An epidemic can strike people of all ages and can cause sudden declines in population. The last worldwide epidemic—in this case, of influenza—occurred between 1918 and 1919. In those years, the flu killed roughly 20 million people around the world.

b. Complete the chart in Activity 2. Then share your group's chart with the class.

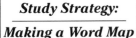

4. **Make a Word Map**

Classwork. Use information from page 125 to complete these word maps. Add your own ideas, too.

Study Strategy:

Making a Word Map

Making a word map is a good way to collect information about a new word.

Example:

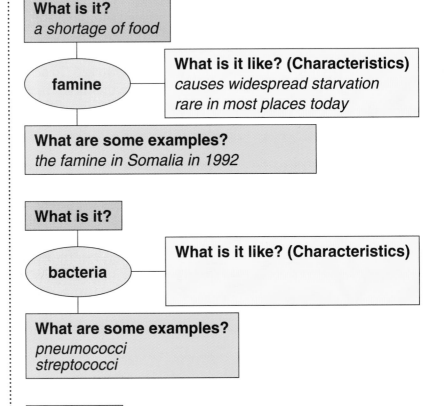

What is it?
a shortage of food

famine

What is it like? (Characteristics)
causes widespread starvation
rare in most places today

What are some examples?
the famine in Somalia in 1992

What is it?

bacteria

What is it like? (Characteristics)

What are some examples?
pneumococci
streptococci

What is it?

epidemic

What is it like? (Characteristics)

What are some examples?

5. Classify

Pairwork. Find these words in the reading on page 125. Use context to guess the meaning of each word. Then put the words into two groups.

bacteria	*harvest*	*sick*
epidemic	*illness*	*starvation*
famine	*infection*	*seeds*

Words related to food   **Words related to disease**

_____   _____

_____   _____

_____   _____

Study Strategy:

Using Context

Use the words and ideas around a new word to guess its meaning.

6. Identify

a. Pairwork. For each pair of sentences, identify the cause and the effect.

1. a. Farmers used new farming methods and better seeds. ___cause___

   b. Farmers were able to grow more food. ___effect___

2. a. The harvests were larger each year. _____

   b. Food became cheaper. _____

3. a. People could send food to different parts of the world. _____

   b. New means of transportation were available. _____

4. a. People could send food to areas without food. _____

   b. Fewer people died of starvation. _____

5. a. Fewer people died. _____

   b. Scientists discovered the cause of some diseases. _____

b. Complete these sentences.

1. Farmers were able to grow more food because

_____.

2. Food became cheaper because _____

_____.

3. People could send food to different parts of the world because _____

_____.

4. Fewer people died of starvation because _____

_____.

5. Fewer people died because _____

_____.

Language Focus:

Identifying Cause and Effect

Farmers were able to grow more food because they used new farming methods.

Language Focus:

Giving Reasons

■ One reason is that _____ .
■ Another reason is that _____ .
■ The most important reason is that _____ .

 7. Write

Groupwork. Take turns writing answers to this question:

Why has the earth's population grown rapidly in the past 150 years?

First student: The most important reason is that

_____.

Second student: Another reason is that _____

_____.

Third student: Another reason is that _____

_____.

8. Share Ideas

Groupwork. Discuss these questions. Then report the results of your discussion to the class.

a. What problems might the increase in population cause?

b. Choose one of the problems from part a. Tell what people can do to solve this problem.

9. Make a Line Graph

a. Groupwork. Use the statistics below to make a line graph.

U.S Population, 1900–1990

Year	Total Population
1900	76,212,168
1910	92,228,496
1920	106,021,537
1930	123,202,624
1940	132,164,569
1950	151,325,798
1960	179,323,175
1970	203,302,031
1980	226,542,203
1990	248,709,873

b. Share your graph with the class.

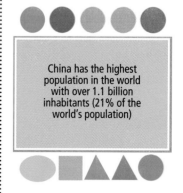

China has the highest population in the world with over 1.1 billion inhabitants (21% of the world's population)

10. Analyze

Groupwork. Use your line graph to answer these questions:

1. In which ten-year period did the population of the United States increase the least? Choose one answer.

   Between 1910 and 1920

   Between 1930 and 1940

   Between 1950 and 1960

2. What effect do you think the events below had on the population of the United States?

The United States entered the First World War. 1918

The United States entered the Second World War. 1959

1917 A flu epidemic killed hundreds of thousands of people in the United States.

1941 Alaska and Hawaii became part of the United States.

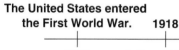

Working for social and political change: Rosa Parks

All citizens in the United States have certain basic rights. If a law unfairly restricts these rights, people can challenge the law, or work to change it. Throughout the history of the United States, people have worked to gain and protect their rights. In this section, you will look at the way one group of people worked to change a law.

 1. Think-Pair-Share

a. On your own. Think about a time when someone treated you unfairly.

- What did they do?
- How did you feel?
- What did you do?

b. Tell your story to a partner. Listen carefully to your partner's story.

c. Get together with another pair. Tell your partner's story.

2. Preview

a. Groupwork. Choose one of the photographs on pages 131–133. Write five questions about the photograph.

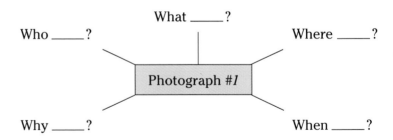

Who ____?

What ____?

Where ____?

Photograph #1

Why ____?

When ____?

b. Share your questions with the class. Together, think of possible answers.

c. The passage on pages 131–133. is about a group of people who wanted to change a law. What law do you think they wanted to change? Use the pictures to make a prediction.

 3. Shared Reading

Read or listen to find answers to your questions.

Taking Action for Change

Before 1964, many places in the United States had laws that segregated, or separated, black and white Americans. These laws forced black Americans to use separate schools, restrooms, restaurants, and other public facilities. Usually, the facilities for black people were not as good as the facilities for white people.

In some cities, black people had to sit in the back of public buses. When the white section in the front of the bus was full, black people had to give their seats to white people.

In 1955, Rosa Parks challenged the unfair bus law in Montgomery, Alabama. When a bus driver asked Rosa Parks to give her seat to a white person, she refused. The police arrested Rosa Parks and took her to jail. In her autobiography, Rosa Parks describes this event:

> One evening in early December 1955 I was sitting in the front seat of the colored section of a bus in Montgomery, Alabama. The white people were sitting in the white section. More white people got on, and they filled up all the seats in the white section. When that happened, we black people were supposed to give up our seats to the whites. But I didn't move. The white driver said, "Let me have those front seats." I didn't get up. I was tired of giving in to white people.
>
> "I'm going to have you arrested," the driver said.
>
> "You may do that," I answered.
>
> Two white policemen came. I asked one of them, "Why do you all push us around?"
>
> He answered, "I don't know, but the law is the law and you're under arrest."

In response to Rosa Parks's arrest, the black citizens of Montgomery, Alabama, decided to boycott the buses. For 381 days, they refused to ride the buses. Instead, they organized car pools or walked to work. By boycotting the buses, they hoped to force the city to change its unfair segregation laws. But the city refused to listen even though the bus company was losing a lot of money.

Thirteen months after the boycott began, the U.S. Supreme Court ruled that segregation in public transportation was unconstitutional. Black people could no longer be forced to sit in the back of buses or give their seats to white people. The day after the segregation laws were changed, Rosa Parks got on a bus and took a seat in the front. It had taken more than a year, but the black people of Montgomery had won a great victory.

Many people were inspired by Rosa Parks's courageous action. They decided to challenge the unfair segregation laws in restaurants, schools, and other public places. In case after case, the Supreme Court ruled that segregation was illegal. Then in 1964, Congress passed a law that forbade segregation in most public facilities. Passage of this law was an important step in protecting the rights of all U.S. citizens.

4. Share Ideas

Classwork. Share ideas about Rosa Parks. Here are some questions to think about:

a. How do you think Rosa Parks felt when the bus driver asked her to move?

b. What effect did Rosa Parks's action have?

c. Why do you think people in Montgomery decided to boycott the buses? What was their goal?

d. What problems do you think the bus boycott caused for the citizens of Montgomery? For the bus company?

e. A heroine is a woman who is admired for her bravery, strength, or goodness. Do you think Rosa Parks is a heroine? Why or why not?

5. Retell

Pairwork. In your own words, tell what Rosa Parks did on December 1, 1955.

6. Define

a. On your own. Choose a word or words to complete each sentence.

brought together/kept apart

1. Many places in the United States had laws that _____ , or separated, black and white Americans. These laws forced black Americans to use separate schools, restrooms, and other public facilities.

agreed with/disagreed with

2. Rosa Parks _____ the unfair bus segregation laws. When a bus driver asked her to give her seat to a white person, she refused.

use/stop using

3. The black citizens of Montgomery decided to _____ the public buses. For 381 days, they refused to ride the buses.

b. Pairwork. Compare sentences. Then answer these questions:

1. What words and ideas in the sentences helped you to choose a word?

2. Find the sentences above in the text on pages 131–133. What words did the writer use? Use context to guess the meaning of these words.

7. Analyze

Classwork. What effect did the actions below have? List your ideas.

CAUSE	EFFECT
Rosa Parks refused to give up her seat.	_____ _____
The police arrested Rosa Parks.	_____ _____
The Supreme Court declared that segregation on public buses was unconstitutional.	_____ _____

Classwork. Here's Rosa Parks's story in the form of a play. Listen and read along.

CAST

Narrator	Passengers on bus (3)
Rosa Parks	First policeman
First woman	Second policeman
Another bystander	Mr. E. D. Nixon
Bus Driver	

The Unexpected Heroine

SCENE 1

NARRATOR: Some historical turning points start out uneventfully. Such is the story of Mrs. Rosa Parks.

FIRST WOMAN: (*approaching bus stop*) Hello, Rosa. How are you?

ROSA PARKS: All right. How are you?

FIRST WOMAN: Fine—just tired after a hard day's work.

ANOTHER BYSTANDER: I hope we can get a seat. It's a shame—the few seats they have for colored people on the bus.

ROSA PARKS: It sure is. Here comes the bus.

NARRATOR: The bus pulls up and the three women get on and pay their fares.

FIRST WOMAN: Just like I thought. There are not many seats left for us. Rosa, you take this one. I'll get one farther back.

ROSA PARKS: Thank you.

▲▲▲

NARRATOR:	Rosa Parks had just started to relax when the bus stopped again and several white passengers got on. Most of the new passengers found seats, but one man was left standing. The bus driver noticed that man and called to Rosa Parks and three other black people sitting beside her and across the aisle from her.
BUS DRIVER:	Let me have those seats.
NARRATOR:	At first, no one stood up. Then the bus driver spoke again.
BUS DRIVER:	You all better make it light on yourselves and give me those seats.
NARRATOR:	The other three people stand up, but Rosa Parks remains seated.
BUS DRIVER:	(*to Rosa Parks*) Are you going to stand?
ROSA PARKS:	No, sir, I'm not.
BUS DRIVER:	If you don't stand up, I'll call the police and have you arrested.
ROSA PARKS:	I understand.
NARRATOR:	With that, the bus driver gets off the bus. Passengers begin whispering to each other.
FIRST PASSENGER:	I wonder what's going to happen.
SECOND PASSENGER:	I don't know.
FIRST PASSENGER:	I'm not going to stay around to find out. I'm getting off this bus.
THIRD PASSENGER:	Look, here comes the bus driver with two policemen.
FIRST POLICEMAN:	(*to Rosa Parks*) Did the driver ask you to stand?

ROSA PARKS:	Yes, he did.
FIRST POLICEMAN:	Well, why didn't you stand?
ROSA PARKS:	I don't think I should have to stand up. Why do you all push us around?
FIRST POLICEMAN:	I don't know, but the law's the law, and you're under arrest.
NARRATOR:	Rosa Parks stands up when the policeman tells her that she is under arrest. They get off the bus and the two policemen walk her to the police car. One carries her purse; the other, her shopping bag.

SCENE 2

NARRATOR:	At the police station, Rosa Parks calls Mr. E. D. Nixon, who is former president of the state and local NAACP.*
ROSA PARKS:	Hello, Mr. Nixon. This is Rosa Parks. I'm calling to let you know that I've been arrested for refusing to give up my bus seat.
MR. E. D. NIXON:	You are one brave woman, Mrs. Parks. I'll be right there to post bail. Then we'll see what we can do.
NARRATOR:	Mrs. Parks was released from jail. Mr. Nixon called Rev. Ralph Abernathy and Rev. Martin Luther King, Jr., and the three started planning the famous bus boycott in Montgomery, Alabama. It was the beginning of the civil rights movement. Eventually, the buses in Montgomery were successfully desegregated.

*NAACP—The NAACP, or National Association for the Advancement of Colored People, was organized in 1910. This organization plays an important role in the modern civil rights movement. Using legal means, it works to gain equal rights for all Americans.

▲▲▲

9. Reader's Theater

Work in groups. Act out *The Unexpected Heroine.*

10. Write

On your own. Follow these instructions to write about someone you admire:

a. List the names of people you admire. (These can be relatives, friends, or famous people.)

b. Choose one person on your list to write about. Think of words and phrases to describe this person.

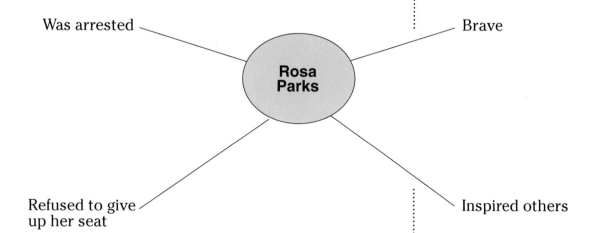

Was arrested

Brave

Rosa Parks

Refused to give up her seat

Inspired others

c. Use your ideas to write a "two-word" poem. Each line in your poem should have only two words. You can write many lines or just a few.

Example: *Rosa Parks*
brave woman
said, "No"
inspired many
to work
for change

d. Share your poem with the class.

Activity Menu

Choose one of the following activities to do.

1. Guess the Year

Find photographs taken at different times in the past. Show your classmates the photographs and ask them to guess the year.

2. What's Changing?

Choose one place to observe at different times during the day (e.g., the school cafeteria, the street on which you live, the view from a window). Record your observations on a chart. In writing, tell how this place changed during the day. Share your writing with the class.

Time of Day	Observations

3. Take a Poll

What invention would you have a hard time living without? Ask ten to twenty students. Record their answers on a bar graph.

4. Who's the Inventor?

Choose an invention that interests you. Look for information to answer the questions in the chart on page 121. Present the results of your research to the class.

5. Illustrate

Choose a device—something that you use every day. Find out how this device works. Then illustrate this device to show your classmates how it works.

▲▲▲

6. Compare Life in the Past with Today

List everything that you use in one day. This might include things like a radio, pencil, and toothbrush. Tell what you used each thing for. The next day, read over your list. Put an X next to the items that were NOT available 100 years ago. For each of these items, tell what you think people used 100 years ago.

7. What's in the Kitchen?

Draw a kitchen as it might look in 1800, 1920, 1992, or 2500. Show the latest inventions of the day.

8. How Fast Does It Grow?

Plant a morning glory seed (or some other fast-growing plant). Take a weekly measurement of its height, and record the data on a line graph. In writing, describe how the plant changed over time.

9. Research

Many people have worked for social and political change in the United States. The list below names just a few of these people. Look in the library for information about one of these people. What did this person try to change? Share your information with the class.

Frederick Douglass   Sojourner Truth
Harriet Tubman   William Lloyd Garrison
Lucretia Mott   Cesar Chavez

10. Learn about the Modern Civil Rights Movement

Collect information about other important events in the modern Civil Rights Movement. Use the information to make a timeline.

11. Is the Population of Your School Changing?

How many students are there in your school this year? How many were there each year for the past ten years? See if your school office has this information. Then make a line graph showing how the population of your school has changed over time. Suggest possible reasons for any changes in population. Then interview someone in your school office for an explanation.

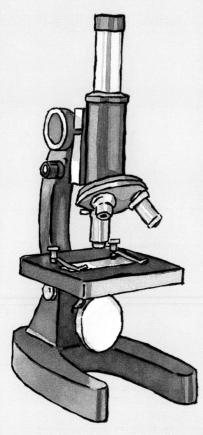

The Microscope

Anton Leeuwenhoek was Dutch.
He sold pincushions, cloth, and such.
The waiting townsfolk fumed and fussed
As Anton's dry goods gathered dust.

He worked, instead of tending store,
At grinding special lenses for
A microscope. Some of the things
He looked at were:
                        mosquitoes' wings
the hairs of sheep, the legs of lice,
the skin of people, dogs, and mice;
ox eyes, spiders' spinning gear,
fishes' scales, a little smear
of his own blood,
                     and best of all,
the unknown, busy, very small
bugs that swim and bump and hop
inside a simple water drop.

Impossible! Most Dutchmen said.
This Anton's crazy in the head.
We ought to ship him off to Spain.
He says he's seen a housefly's brain.
He says the water that we drink
Is full of bugs. He's mad, we think!

They called him *dumkopf*, which means dope.
That's how we got the microscope.

—*Maxine Kumin*

Change

The summer
still hangs
heavy and sweet
with sunlight
as it did last year.

The autumn
still comes
showering
gold and crimson
as it did last year.

The winter
still stings
clean and
cold and white
as it did last year.

The spring
still comes
like a whisper
in the dark night.

It is only I
who have changed.

—*Charlotte Zolotow*

What's the conflict? ▶

Finding a win-win solution: peer mediation
▼

Making peace: The Iroquois Confederacy

Dealing with conflict:

A poem ▶

◀ A folktale

RESOLVING CONFLICT

◀ Looking at both sides of a conflict ▶

A: I think it was a good movie.
B: I didn't like it at all. ▶

▲ The American Civil War lasted for four years.
During this conflict, more than 600,000 people died.

What's the Conflict?

1. Write a Definition

a. Classwork. What is conflict? Study the pictures and captions and write a definition.

b. Look up the word *conflict* in a dictionary. Write the dictionary definition.

c. How is your definition similar to the dictionary? Different?

The soccer game is at three o'clock today and so is my music lesson. ▼

◀ A: I want you to babysit your brother this afternoon.

B: But I want ▶ to go out with my friends.

2. Listen

a. Classwork. Listen to the three dialogues and answer the question below.

Dialogue	What is the conflict?
1	One person wants to go outside. The other person _____.
2	One person _____. The other person _____.
3	One person _____. The other person _____.

b. Classwork. Listen to the dialogues again. How is the third dialogue different? Share ideas with your classmates.

3. Quickwrite

Study Strategy:

Quickwriting

Quickwriting is a good way to explore ideas. When you quick-write, try to write without stopping.

a. On your own. Think about a time when you disagreed with someone. Quickwrite about this disagreement for five minutes. Here are some questions you might think about:

- Who did you disagree with?
- What was the disagreement about?
- What happened in the end?
- How did you feel in the end?

b. Share ideas from your quickwriting with a classmate.

▲▲▲

Dealing with conflict: A folktale

People deal with conflict in different ways. In the folktale on page 153, two people have a disagreement. When you read the story, you will find out how they deal with conflict.

1. Analyze

Classwork. Study the cartoon and answer these questions:

a. What do the two donkeys want to do?
b. What problem do they have?
c. How do they solve the problem?

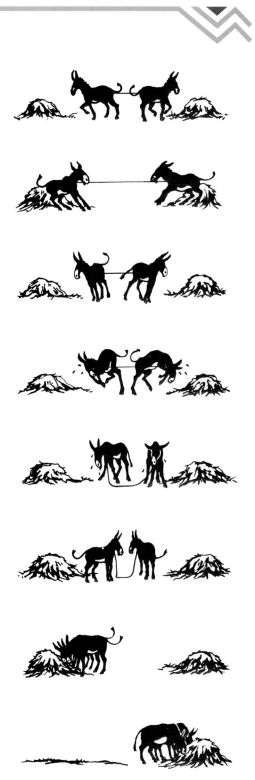

a. Classwork. Look again at the cartoon. What is the conflict?

b. How did the donkeys in the cartoon deal with the conflict? Choose one of the ways shown in the diagram below.

They put off talking about the conflict until they are both calm.

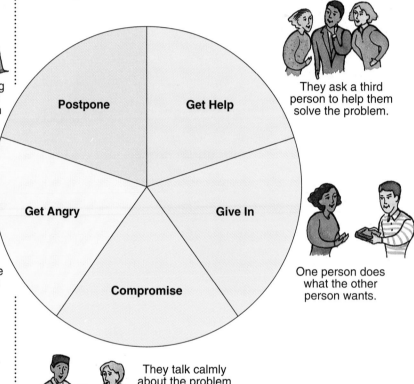

They ask a third person to help them solve the problem.

Postpone

Get Help

Get Angry

Give In

Compromise

They insist they are right and refuse to listen to the other person.

One person does what the other person wants.

They talk calmly about the problem and find a solution that makes both people happy.

c. Groupwork. Listen to the four dialogues on page 151. Then read them and follow these steps.

1. Identify the conflict.
2. Tell how the people deal with the conflict. (Use the diagram above for ideas.)
3. Share your ideas with the class.

Dialogue

1. A: Let's go somewhere.
   B: No, I don't want to.
   A: Why? Are you tired?
   B: Yeah.
   A: OK. Then let's stay here.

2. A: Can I read the story aloud?
   B: Well, I really wanted to.
   A: Then you read the first half and I'll read the second half.
   B: OK.

3. A: Why didn't you call me?
   B: I did call, but you weren't home.
   A: I don't believe you.
   B: It's true.
   A: OK. OK. I'm going to go for a walk. Let's talk about it later.

4. A: I think we should invite everyone to the party.
   B: We can't do that. That's too many people.
   A: So what?
   B: But we won't have enough food.
   A: Are you sure? Let's see what Julia thinks.

Dialogue	How do they deal with the conflict?
1	_____
2	_____
3	_____
4	_____

3. Predict

Classwork. In the story *Stewed, Roasted, and Live?*, two people have a disagreement. Think about the title of the story. What do you think the disagreement is about?

Stewed and roasted are ways to cook food.

Stewed tomatoes   *Roast chicken*

4. Preview

a. Groupwork. Choose one of the pictures on page 153. Write five questions about the picture.

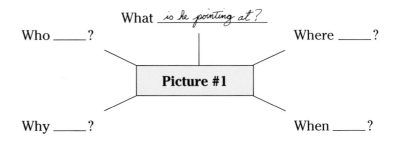

Who _____ ?   What *is he pointing at?*   Where _____ ?

Picture #1

Why _____ ?   When _____ ?

b. Share your group's questions with the class. Together, think of possible answers.

Stewed, Roasted, or Live?
(A Chinese Folktale)

Two hunters were in the field all day. They were about to go home when they suddenly saw a flock of wild geese. Quick as a wink, they took out their bows and arrows and waited for the geese to fly overhead.

"They are very fat geese," said one hunter, licking his lips. "Think of it . . . stewed goose."

"Or roasted," said the other hunter. "I really like roasted goose."

"Stewed goose is better!"

"Oh, no. Roasted goose is better!" The first hunter looked angrily at his friend. His voice got louder. "Stewed!"

The second hunter looked angrily back at his friend. "ROASTED!" They glared at each other.

"Stewed!"

"Roasted!"

The two hunters stared angrily at each other for a long minute. Then they turned away and raised their bows to the sky once more.

But the geese were already far away.

◆ **6.** Share Ideas

Classwork. What's your reaction to the story? Discuss ideas with your classmates. Here are some other questions to think about:

a. Did you like this story? Why or why not?

b. What did the two hunters disagree about?

c. How did the two hunters deal with the conflict? Do you think this was a good way?

d. Folktales often try to teach something. What do you think this folktale is supposed to teach?

◆ **7.** Make a Story Map

a. Pairwork. Use information from the story to make a story map.

Stewed, Roasted, or Live?

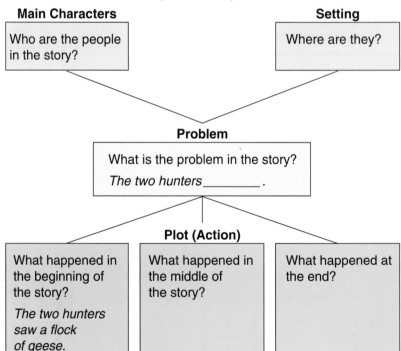

Main Characters

Who are the people in the story?

Setting

Where are they?

Problem

What is the problem in the story?

The two hunters_____.

Plot (Action)

What happened in the beginning of the story?

The two hunters saw a flock of geese.

What happened in the middle of the story?

What happened at the end?

b. Compare story maps with classmates.

 **8.** Roleplay

Groupwork. Work in groups of three. Act out the story *Stewed, Roasted, or Live?*. Two people are the hunters in the story. One person is the narrator. Practice first. Then perform for the class.

 **9.** Write

a. On your own. Choose one of these activities:

1. Imagine that you are one of the hunters. Write about what happened today. Tell how you feel about it.
2. Add to the story *Stewed, Roasted,* or *Live?*. Tell what the hunters did next.

b. Share your writing with the class.

 **10.** Write

a. Pairwork. Choose one of these ways of dealing with conflict:

      compromise   give in   postpone

Write a new dialogue for the story. Show how the two hunters deal with the conflict in a different way.

New Dialogue

A: They are very fat geese.

    Think of it . . . stewed goose.

B: _____

A: _____

b. Share your dialogue with the class.

In some cultures, a dove symbolizes peace.

Dealing with conflict:
A poem

Language Focus:

Relating Cause and Effect

- If a friend called me a name, I would feel unhappy.
- If a friend _____ , I would feel miserable.

When people get angry, they sometimes say things that hurt other people. That's what the poem in this section is about.

 Identify

Classwork. Read the title of the poem below. What might a friend do or say that would make you feel miserable, or very unhappy? Share ideas with your classmates.

calls me a name

```
( a friend's action ) — ( things that would make me feel miserable ) — ( a friend's words )
```

 Shared Reading

Read this poem aloud several times.

Misery

Misery is when your
very best friend
calls you a name she really
didn't mean to call you at all.

Misery is when you call
your very best friend a name
you didn't mean to call her, either.

—*Langston Hughes*

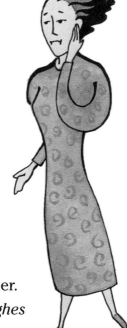

8. Roleplay

Groupwork. Work in groups of three. Act out the story *Stewed, Roasted, or Live?*. Two people are the hunters in the story. One person is the narrator. Practice first. Then perform for the class.

9. Write

a. On your own. Choose one of these activities:

1. Imagine that you are one of the hunters. Write about what happened today. Tell how you feel about it.

2. Add to the story *Stewed, Roasted,* or *Live?*. Tell what the hunters did next.

b. Share your writing with the class.

10. Write

a. Pairwork. Choose one of these ways of dealing with conflict:

> compromise   give in   postpone

Write a new dialogue for the story. Show how the two hunters deal with the conflict in a different way.

New Dialogue

A: They are very fat geese.

    Think of it . . . stewed goose.

B: _____

A: _____

b. Share your dialogue with the class.

In some cultures, a dove symbolizes peace.

Dealing with conflict: A poem

Language Focus:

Relating Cause and Effect

- If a friend called me a name, I would feel unhappy.
- If a friend _____ , I would feel miserable.

When people get angry, they sometimes say things that hurt other people. That's what the poem in this section is about.

1. **Identify**

Classwork. Read the title of the poem below. What might a friend do or say that would make you feel miserable, or very unhappy? Share ideas with your classmates.

calls me a name

(a friend's action) — (things that would make me feel miserable) — (a friend's words)

2. **Shared Reading**

Read this poem aloud several times.

Misery

Misery is when your
very best friend
calls you a name she really
didn't mean to call you at all.

Misery is when you call
your very best friend a name
you didn't mean to call her, either.

—*Langston Hughes*

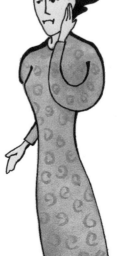

3. Share Ideas

Classwork. Share ideas about the poem with your classmates. Here are some questions that you might think about.

a. What is "misery" to the poet? Do you agree or disagree?

b. Why do you think a friend might call you a name?

c. How would you feel if someone called you a name? What would you do?

d. Do you think name-calling is a good way to deal with conflict? Why or why not?

4. Write

a. Groupwork. Choose an idea from your cluster diagram in Activity 1. Use this idea to write a poem.

Misery is when _____

_____

_____

_____

_____.

Misery is when you _____

_____

_____

_____

_____.

b. Read your poem to the class.

The best way to resolve a conflict is to find a solution that makes everyone happy. That's a win-win solution. In this section, you will read about some strategies for finding a win-win solution.

1. **Identify**

a. Groupwork. Read or listen to these stories and answer the questions in the chart.

1. Shawn and Leila are working together on a class project. They have to write a report about a famous person in history. Shawn wants to write about Rosa Parks because he's interested in the Civil Rights Movement. Leila has already read a lot about Rosa Parks, and she wants to write about someone different. After talking about it, they decide to write about Martin Luther King, Jr., a leader in the Civil Rights Movement.

2. Marta and Yan have to interview people outside school and then make a report to the class. Yan suggests that they do the interviews together after school, but Marta says she can't. Yan gets angry because he doesn't want to do all the work. He tells Marta that she is lazy. Marta tries to tell Yan that she can't do the interviews because she has to babysit after school. But Yan refuses to listen. He says he'll do the work himself, and then he walks away.

	Shawn and Leila	Marta and Yan
What is the conflict?		
How do they deal with the conflict?		
What solution do they reach?		

b. Classwork. A win-win solution allows both people to feel good. Which of the solutions above is a win-win solution? Why?

2. Analyze

Classwork. Read the title of the article on page 160 and study the picture. What do you think the students in the picture are discussing? Share ideas with your classmates.

Finding a Win-Win Solution

Two students started arguing at school. One student called the other one a name, and a fistfight began.

What can be done to prevent fights like this at school? In some schools, the disputants (the two students with a disagreement) sit down with peer mediators. Peer mediators are students with special training in conflict resolution.

Peer mediators help the disputants to communicate peacefully. Here are some of the communication strategies they use:

1. State your own feelings clearly but don't be accusatory. Begin with "I feel . . ." instead of "You always . . ."
2. Don't interrupt or finish another person's sentences.
3. Listen carefully to what the other person is saying. Try to see the other person's side of the disagreement.
4. Maintain eye contact with the other person.
5. Ask questions to make sure that you understand the other person.

6. Repeat the other person's ideas as you understand them.

7. Never put anyone down. Saying things like "You're stupid" makes communication difficult.

8. Try to find a solution that makes both people happy.

Peer mediators never judge the disputants. They don't decide who is right and who is wrong. Instead, they help the two students to find their own "win-win" solution. A "win-win" solution allows everyone to feel good.

Peer mediation often succeeds simply because it gets people to talk to each other. And getting people to communicate is the first step in finding a win-win solution.

More than 2,000 schools in the United States now have conflict resolution programs for students.

4. Identify

a. On your own. Decide if these sentences are true or false.

	True	False
1. Peer mediators are usually teachers.	___	___
2. Disputants are people with a disagreement.	___	___
3. "I feel angry" is an example of an accusation.	___	___
3. "You're lazy" is an example of a put-down.	___	___
3. Peer mediators find a"win-win" solution for the disputants.	___	___
4. The disputants decide who is right and who is wrong.	___	___
5. Peer mediators help other people to communicate clearly.	___	___

Language Focus:

Agreeing

▪ It's true that disputants are people with a disagreement.

▪ It's true that
_____.

b. Compare ideas with a partner. Show where you found the information in the reading.

c. Report your *True* answers to the class. Rewrite the false statements to make them true.

5. Share Ideas

Classwork. Share ideas about the reading with your classmates. Here are some questions you might think about:

a. Do you think peer mediation is a good way to resolve conflict at school? Why or why not?

b. Would it be easier to discuss your feelings with a peer or with a teacher? Why?

c. Do you think it is difficult to be a peer mediator? Why or why not?

d. Why is it important to understand the other person's side of the conflict?

e. Why is it a good idea to find a win-win solution to a conflict?

6. Evaluate

a. Pairwork. Listen to this dialogue. Then read it aloud.

Shawn and Leila have to write a report about a famous person in history. Here's what happens when they try to choose a person to write about:

Shawn: Why don't we write about Rosa Parks?

Leila: Can't we write about someone else?

Shawn: Why?

Leila: I've already read a lot about Rosa Parks. I'd like to learn about someone different.

Shawn: But I'm really interested in the Civil Rights Movement.

Leila: So you want to write about the Civil Rights Movement?

Shawn: Yeah.

Leila: Well, could we write about someone else in the Civil Rights Movement?

Shawn: I suppose so. Like who?

Leila: What about Martin Luther King, Jr., or Ralph Abernathy?

Shawn: OK. Sounds good to me.

b. Pairwork. Tell which communication strategies Shawn and Leila use.

Communication Strategies	Shawn	Leila
States his or her feelings. Doesn't interrupt. Listens carefully. Tries to see the other person's side. Asks questions. Repeats the other person's ideas. Doesn't put the other person down. Tries to find a win-win solution.		

7. Apply

a. Pairwork. Listen to this dialogue. Then read it aloud and answer the questions on page 164.

Yan and Marta have to do a school project together. For this project, they have to interview people outside school. Here's what happens when they discuss the project:

Yan: Let's do the interviews today.

Marta: I can't, Yan.

Yan: Come on. We have to get the information.

Marta: I know but I . . .

Yan: You know, Marta, you never want to help. You're lazy.

Marta: That's not true. You don't understand. I . . .

Yan: I do understand. I understand that I have to do all the work.

1. Who was accusatory? _____

2. Who interrupted the other person? _____

3. Who put down the other person? _____

   How? _____

b. Pairwork. Rewrite the dialogue. Make sure Yan and Marta follow the communication strategies on page 163.

c. Read your dialogue to the class.

8. **Self-evaluate**

On your own. What strategies do you use when you disagree with someone? Complete an evaluation chart.

	Always	Usually	Sometimes	Never
I state my feelings clearly.				
I avoid accusing the other person.				
I avoid interrupting the other person.				
I look at the other person.				
I ask questions to make sure I understand the other person.				
I repeat the other person's ideas.				
I avoid putting down the other person.				
I try to find a win-win solution.				

▲▲▲

It's impossible to find a win-win solution to a conflict if you don't know what the other person is thinking and feeling. In this section, you will find out how two people think and feel about a conflict.

1. Quickwrite

a. On your own. Look back at your quickwriting from page 148. Write about the disagreement again, but this time write from the other person's point of view.
b. What was easy or difficult about this assignment? Share ideas with your classmates.

2. Shared Reading

Pairwork. Choose one of the conflict situations from pages 165–166. Read or listen to both sides of the story.

Two Sides of a Conflict

Laurie's side of the story:
There's a guy in my class who can't pronounce my last name. No one else has trouble saying it, but he gets it wrong every time. I think he says it wrong on purpose. I try to laugh about it, but it really makes me angry.

Mario's side of the story:
There's a new student at school. She has a real long last name, and I can't pronounce it correctly. I feel stupid because every time I say her name, I get it wrong. She laughs when I say it wrong, so I guess it doesn't matter.

Rigoberto's side of the story:
I don't understand my friends Don and Mark. I've been eating lunch with them at school for two years. Now my friend Carl wants to eat with us, but Don and Mark don't want him to. Carl is not like everybody else—he has learning problems. But he's on the soccer team with me, and he's my friend. Why can't Don and Mark accept him, too? Now I'm afraid Carl and I won't have anyone to eat with.

Don's side of the story:
What is Rigoberto trying to do? We have this nice group of guys who always eat together. Why does Rigoberto have to invite Carl to eat with us? Carl makes us feel uncomfortable, and some kids are always making fun of him. They'll probably make fun of us now.

 3. Report

a. Pairwork. Retell each person's side of the story. Take turns reporting an idea.

b. Get together with another pair. Tell them both sides of the story. Listen to their story.

4. Write

a. Pairwork. Write a dialogue in which the two people try to find a win-win solution to the conflict.

b. Get together with another pair. Listen to their dialogue. Identify their communication strategies.

Language Focus:

Reporting Someone's Ideas

- Laurie says that a guy in her class can't pronounce her name.
- She says that he gets it wrong every time.

	Laurie	Mario
States his or her feelings.		
Doesn't interrupt.		
Listens carefully.		
Tries to see the other person's side.		
Asks questions.		
Repeats the other person's ideas.		
Doesn't put the other person down.		
Tries to find a win-win solution.		

A plan for peace

For many years, the Iroquois people fought among themselves. But in the 1400s, a remarkable plan for peace ended the fighting. In this section, you will read about the Iroquois plan for peace.

1. Define

Groupwork. Complete the sentences below:

Examples: *Peace is a lion and a lamb living together!*
Peace is the world without war.

Peace is _____ .
Peace is _____ .
Peace is _____ .

2. Make a K-W-L Chart

Classwork. Use the pictures and captions on pages 168–169 to make a K-W-L chart.

Answers these questions before you read the story.

Answer this question after you read the story.

Know	Want to Know	Learned
What do you know about the Iroquois people from the pictures?	What do you want to find out?	What did you learn?

Study Strategy:

Making a K-W-L Chart

Making a K-W-L chart is a good way to get ready to read.

A Plan for Peace

Six hundred years ago, five tribes of the Iroquois people lived in the area south of Lake Ontario. The people in these five tribes were similar in a number of ways. They spoke closely related languages. They had similar religious beliefs. They lived in villages and farmed the land. Despite these similarities, conflict among the tribes was common. Sometimes these conflicts erupted into warfare.

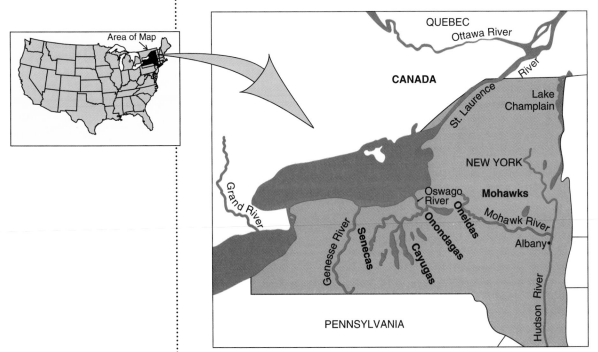

Six hundred years ago, five tribes of Iroquois people lived south of Lake Ontario. Today, this area is part of the state of New York.

One reason for the fighting was a custom known as blood revenge. If someone in one tribe killed a person in another tribe, that person's family had to seek revenge—they had to kill someone in the other person's family. As long as the blood revenge custom existed, there could never be peace among the tribes.

Iroquois people lived in villages and farmed the land. Each village was made up of a number of longhouses. Many families lived together in a longhouse.

According to legend, a wise person known as the Great Peacemaker found a way to bring peace to the tribes. He convinced the tribes to join together in a confederacy, or family of tribes. The confederacy was a permanent form of government designed to help the tribes live together in peace.

The Iroquois Confederacy had a constitution, or set of laws. According to the constitution, each tribe continued to govern itself. To settle disputes between tribes, however, the constitution set up a Great Council. The Council was made up of representatives from each tribe. These representatives were called sachems, or peace chiefs. All of the sachems were men, but they were chosen and advised by women in each tribe.

The Great Council met at least once a year to resolve conflicts and to make new laws. Each sachem could express his opinion to the Council. If there was disagreement, the sachems tried to reach a compromise. No decision could be made until everyone agreed.

There are 20,200 Iroquois people in the U.S. and Canada.

The Iroquois Confederacy was the first form of democracy in North America. Many people believe it was a model for the government of the United States. In the U.S. government, for example, each state sends representatives to the U.S. Congress. This is similar to the government of the Iroquois Confederacy.

The Great Council of the Iroquois Confederacy continues to meet each year. As in the past, it works to solve problems and resolve conflicts peacefully.

 4. **Take Notes in a Chart**

Pairwork. Look back at the reading and take notes in a chart.

Paragraph	Topic (What's the paragraph about?)	Details and Examples
1	description of the Iroquois tribes	▪ lived south of Lake Ontario ▪ were similar in many ways ▪ there was conflict between tribes
2	reason for fighting	
3	plan for peace	
4		
5		

 5. **Test Your Knowledge**

Pairwork. Get together with another pair. Take turns asking and answering questions about the information in your chart.

Example: Q: *Where did the Iroquois people live?*

A: *South of Lake Ontario.*

Study Strategy:

Taking Notes

When you take notes, write only the most important ideas.

Language Focus:

Asking For and Giving Information About the Past

Q: Where did the Iroquois people live?
A: South of Lake Ontario.

Q: Were the tribes similar?
A: Yes, they were.

6. Write

Groupwork. Follow these steps:

a. Write three true sentences about the Iroquois Confederacy.
b. Write three false sentences about the Iroquois Confederacy.
c. Mix up your sentences.
d. Read your sentences to the class. Ask your classmates to identify the true sentences.

7. Make a Word Map

Pairwork. Use information from pages 168–170 to complete these word maps. Add your own ideas, too.

Study Strategy:

Making a Word Map

Making a word map is a good way to collect information about a new word.

Iroquois Confederacy

Definition (What was it?)	Purpose (What was it for?)	Characteristics (What was it like?)
a family of tribes a form of government		

sachems

Definition (What were they?)	Purpose (What were they for?)	Characteristics (How would you describe them?)

Great Council

Definition (What was it?)	Purpose (What was it for?)	Characteristics (What was it like?)

a. Groupwork. Tell about the Iroquois Confederacy and the U.S. government. Complete a chart like this one.

	Iroquois Confederacy	U.S. Government
has a constitution		✔
is a democracy (people have a voice in government)		
is a representative democracy (people elect representatives)		
is a federal system (groups join under central government)		

b. Compare the Iroquois Confederacy and the U.S. Government. Write several sentences.

_____

_____

_____

_____

_____

_____

_____

_____

_____

_____

_____

_____

Language Focus:

Making Comparisons

- Both governments have a constitution.
- The Iroquois government has a constitution and so does the U.S. government.

Apply

Groupwork. In the Great Council of the Iroquois Confederacy, everyone had to agree on a decision. Try this activity to see if you can agree on a decision.

1. Your group can have the four items in the picture below. Think of different ways to share these items among the people in your group.

2. Choose one way to share the items. Make sure everyone in your group is happy with the final decision.
3. Report your decision to the class.

Activity Menu

Choose one of the following activities to do.

1. Make a Collage

How does a peaceful world look? Collect magazine pictures that suggest a peaceful world to you. Use them to make a collage.

2. Choose a Peacemaker

There are many monuments to wars and war heroes. Now, the National Foundation for Peace in Washington, D.C. wants to build monuments to peace and peace heroes. Can you suggest an individual, group, or event that represents peace? Write a description of your representative of peace and tell how the monument might look.

3. Design a Game

Many games and sports are competitive—there is a winner and a loser. A more cooperative type of game allows everyone to win. Design a game in which everyone wins, and teach it to your classmates. You might think of a new type of game or rewrite the rules of an old game.

4. Read a Children's Book

A popular children's book by Katherine Scholes is called *Peace Begins With You.* For ten minutes, think about the title of the book. What ideas would you include in a book with this title? List your ideas. Then read the book to compare ideas with the author.

5. Analyze a TV Program

Watch for an example of conflict in a TV program. Take notes on the cause of conflict and how it is resolved. Then suggest other ways the conflict might be resolved.

6. Design a Peace Symbol

The dove is one symbol of peace. What are some other symbols of peace? Draw pictures of them, then design a new symbol for peace.

7. Write about a Conflict

Describe a conflict between two people. Tell each person's side of the conflict. Let your classmates read your story and suggest a win-win solution.

8. Read a Folktale

Choose another folktale and read it to your classmates. Together, make a story map telling about the folktale.

Read on . . .

Sharing a Culture

Cindy knows that understanding between cultures is at the root of peace. So she started studying under her grandmother to learn all about her own culture—the Oneida Indian Nation, part of the Iroquois Nation. Now she visits schools in New York state, sharing Iroquois songs and stories. One of her favorite stories is about the white pine, planted by the Great Peacemaker who directed the people to bury their weapons at its roots. To honor this message and to bring peace to the environment, Cindy and other Oneida children planted 1,200 white pines on the Oneida Nation Territory. "Planting trees brings us oxygen, holds more soil, and gives animals more homes," she explains.

Law of the Great Peace

I now uproot the tallest tree, and into the hole thereby made, we cast all weapons of war. Into the depths of the earth, down into the deep underneath currents of water flowing to unknown regions, we cast all the weapons of strife. We bury them from sight and we plant again the tree. Thus shall the Great Peace be established, and hostilities shall no longer be known between the Five Nations, but peace to the united people.

A Kingdom Lost for a Drop of Honey
(A Burmese Folktale)

One day the King and his chief minister were standing by the palace window, eating roasted rice and honey. They laughed so much that they spilled some honey on the windowsill.

"We have spilled some honey, Your Majesty," said the chief minister. "Let me wipe it off."

"My dear chief minister," laughed the king, "you are an important person. It is beneath your dignity to do it. And if we call a servant to wipe it away, he will disturb our pleasant conversation. So leave the spilt honey alone."

They went on eating and laughing while a drop of honey dripped down the windowsill onto the street below.

"Chief Minister," said the king, leaning forward, "a drop of the honey has fallen on the street and a fly is now eating it."

The chief minister looked and saw a spider attacking the fly. The king looked down again and saw a lizard eating the spider. The king and minister continued to eat and laugh and soon they saw a cat eating the lizard.

When a dog attacked the cat, they did not stop laughing and eating. They did not stop laughing even when they saw the owner of the cat and the owner of the dog arguing and fighting.

Soon friends of both sides joined in the fight. Still the king and his minister continued to laugh and eat. Before long the fighting spread to other streets. Only then did the king order the palace guards to stop the fighting. However, by that time, the palace guards had also joined the fight, as some of them supported the owner of the dog while others supported the owner of the cat.

In the next few hours, civil war broke out and the palace was destroyed together with the king and the chief minister.

A group of judges went to the Princess Learned-in-the-Law and asked for her advice. She listened to their story and then she said: "My Lord Justices, remember that there is no such thing as a minor disagreement. You must never wait and do nothing. You must deal with each conflict right away, no matter how unimportant it may be. Remember always, my Lords, the story of the kingdom which was lost because of one drop of honey."

Burmese Folktale

Additional Resources

Choosing Foods

Merriam, Eve. *How to Eat a Poem* in *A Sky Full of Poems*. Dell Publishing, 1986.

Soto, Gary. *Ode to La Tortilla* and *Ode to Pomegranates* in *Neighborhood Odes*. Harcourt Brace Jovanovich.

Jones, Mary Ellen. *Seeds of Change, Readings on Cultural Exchange after 1492*. Addison-Wesley, 1993.

Perl, Lila. *Junk Food, Fast Food, Health Food*. Houghton Mifflin, 1980.

Tatchell, Judy, and Wells, Dilys. *You and Your Food*. Usborne Publishers, 1985.

Life Science Library. *Food and Nutrition.* Time Inc.

International Food Library. Rourke Publishing.

Ontario Science Center. *Foodworks*. Addison-Wesley.

Copp, Vicki. *Science Experiments You Can Eat*. Harper and Row, 1972.

Albynt, Carole Lisa, and Sihaiko Webb, Lois. *The Multicultural Cookbook for Students*. Oryx Press, 1993.

Sending Messages

Baylor, Byrd, comp. *Why Dogs Don't Talk Anymore* in *And It Is Still That Way, Legends told by Arizona Indian Children*. Trails West Publishing, 1976.

Selected and Adapted in Spanish by José Griego y Maestas. Retold in English by Rudolpho A. Anaya. *The Man Who Knew the Language of Animals* in *Cuentos, Tales from the Hispanic Southwest*. The Museum of New Mexico Press, 1980.

Hayes, Joe. *La Llorona* (The Crying Woman) in *The Day It Snowed Tortillas, Tales from Spanish New Mexico*. Mariposa Publishing, 1990.

Krashe, Robert. *The Twelve Million Dollar Note: Strange but True Tales of Messages Found in Seagoing Bottles*. Thomas Nelson Publishers, 1977.

Ardley, Neil. *Music*. Eyewitness Books, Alfred A. Knopf, 1989.

How Animals Behave. Books for World Explorers, National Geographic Society, 1984.

Mountfield, Anne. *Looking Back at Sending Messages*. Schoolhouse Press, Needham, 1988.

Musical Instruments of the World. Facts on File, 1976.

Setting Goals

Spier, Peter. *We the People, the Constitution, and the United States of America*. Doubleday and Company, 1987.

Faber, Doris and Harold. *We the People*. Charles Scribner, 1987.

Johnson, Neil. *All in a Day's Work*. Little, Brown, and Company, 1989.

Westridge Young Writers Workshop. *Kid's Explore America's Hispanic Heritage*. Jon Muir Publications, 1992.

Berry, Joy. *Every Kid's Guide to Laws That Relate to School and Work*. Children's Press, 1987.

Schleifer, Jay. *Citizenship*. Rosen Publishing Group, Inc., 1990.

Career Discovery Encyclopedia. Volumes 1–6. Ferguson Publishing Company, 1990.

Bolles, Richard Nelson. *What Color Is Your Parachute?* Ten Speed Press, 1993.

VGM Careers for You Series, VGM Career Horizons. NTC Publishing Group, 1991.

Making Changes

Parks, Rosa. *Rosa Parks: My Story*. Dial Books.

Greenfield, Eloise. *Rosa Parks*. Crowell, 1973.

Myers, Walter Dean. *Now Is Your Time! The African-American Struggle for Freedom*. HarperCollins, 1991.

America's Civil Rights Movement, Teaching Kit. One free kit available per school upon written request from school principal. Send request to The Southern Poverty Law Center, Teaching Tolerance Project, 400 Washington Avenue, Montgomery, Alabama, 36104.

Roché, Joyce M., and Rodriguez, Marie. *Kids Who Make a Difference*. Mastermedia Limited, 1993.

Haber, Louis. *Black Pioneers of Science and Invention*. An Odyssey Book, Harcourt Brace Jovanovich, 1970.

Inventors and Discoverers, Changing Our World. National Geographic Society, 1988.

Panati, Charles. *Extraordinary Origins of Everyday Things*. Harper and Row, 1987.

Buchman, Dian Dincin, and Groves, Seli. *What If? Fifty Discoveries That Changed the World*. Scholastic Inc., 1988.

Winckler, Suzanne, and Rodgers, Mary M. *Population Growth*. Lerner Publications Company, 1991.

Resolving Conflict

Courlander, Harold, and Herzog, George. *Guinea Fowl and Rabbit Get Justice* in *The Cow Tail Switch and Other West African Stories*. Henry Holt and Company, 1947.

Teaching Tolerance (educational journal for teachers). Free subscription available upon written request to The Southern Poverty Law Center, Teaching Tolerance Project, 400 Washington Avenue, Montgomery, Alabama, 36104.

George, Phil. *Battle Won Is Lost* in *The Whispering Wind, Poetry by Young American Indians*. Edited by Terry Allen. Doubleday.

Exley, Richard and Helen, eds. *My World Peace, Thoughts and Illustrations from the Children of All Nations*. Passport Books, National Textbook Company, 1985.

Harrison, Michael, and Stuart-Clark, Christopher, comp. *Peace and War, A Collection of Poems*. Oxford University Press.

▲▲▲

Junne, I.K., ed. *Two Foolish Friends* in *Floating Clouds, Floating Dreams, Favorite Asian Folktales*. Doubleday.

Htin Aung, Maung, and Trager, Helen G. *Partnership* in *A Kingdom Lost for a Drop of Honey* and *Other Burmese Folktales*. Parents Magazine Press.

Durell, Ann, and Sachs, Marilyn, eds. *The Big Book for Peace*. Dutton Children's Books, 1990.

McCall, Barbara. *The Iroquois*. Rourke Publications, 1989.

Text permissions

We wish to thank the authors, publishers, and holders of copyright for their permission to reprint the following:

Black Misery by Langston Hughes. Copyright © 1969 by Langston Hughes. Reprinted by permission of Harold Ober Associates, Inc.

Bouki's Glasses from *The Piece of Fire and Other Haitian Tales* by Harold Courlander. Copyright © 1964 by Harold Courlander. Reprinted by permission of the author.

Change by Charlotte Zolotow from *River Winding*. Copyright © 1970 by Charlotte Zolotow. Reprinted by permission of the author and Edite Kroll Literary Agency.

David Klein by Mel Glenn from *Class Dismissed II*. Text copyright © 1986 by Mel Glenn. Reprinted by permission of Clarion Books/Houghton Mifflin Company. All rights reserved.

Deaf Donald by Shel Silverstein from *A Light in the Attic*. Copyright © 1981 by Shel Silverstein. Reprinted by permission of HarperCollins Publishers and Edite Kroll Literary Agency.

Devices That Help the Deaf by the students of the Horace Mann School for the Deaf in Allston, MA, and Marie Franklin, editor of The Fun Pages. Copyright © 1992 by the *Boston Globe*. Reprinted by permission of the *Boston Globe*.

Homero E. Acevedo II from *Kids Explore America's Hispanic Heritage*. Copyright © 1992 by John Muir Publications. Reprinted by permission of John Muir Publications.

How Do You Eat a Hot Fudge Sundae by Jonathan Holden from *Design for a House: Poems*. Copyright © 1972 by Jonathan Holden. Reprinted by permission of the University of Missouri Press.

How to Eat a Poem by Eve Merriam from *A Sky Full of Poems*. Copyright © 1964, 1970, 1973 by Eve Merriam. Reprinted by permission of Marian Reiner.

An Immigrant in the U.S. by Ponn Pet, age 11, from *Stone Soup, the magazine by children*. Copyright © 1990 by the Children's Art Foundation, Santa Cruz, California.

A Kingdom Lost for a Drop of Honey adapted by Helen G. Trager and Maung Htlin from *A Kingdom Lost for a Drop of Honey and Other Burmese Folk-Tales*. Reprinted by permission of Scholastic, Inc.

Law of the Great Peace adapted by John Bierhorst from *The Iroquois Book of the Great Law*. Copyright © by John Bierhorst. Reprinted by permission of John Bierhorst.

The Microscope by Maxine Kumin. Copyright © 1963 by Maxine Kumin. First published in *The Atlantic Monthly*. Reprinted by permission of Curtis Brown, Ltd.

From *My Story* by Rosa Parks. Copyright © 1992 by Rosa Parks. Published by Dial Books.

From *Our Endangered Planet: Population Growth* by Suzanne Winckler and Mary M. Rogers. Copyright © 1991 by Lerner Publications Company, Minneapolis, MN. Used with permission. All rights reserved.

A Round by Eve Merriam from *A Sky Full of Poems*. Copyright © 1964, 1970, 1973 by Eve Merriam. Reprinted by permission of Marian Reiner.

Sharing a Culture from *Learning Magazine*, November/December 1992. Copyright © 1992 by *Learning Magazine*. Reprinted by permission of *Learning Magazine*.

The Unexpected Heroine from *Take a Walk in Their Shoes* by Glennette Tilley Turner. Copyright © 1989 by Glennette Tilley Turner. Used by permission of Cobblehill Books, an affiliate of Dutton Children's Books, a division of Penguin USA, Inc.

That's Nice by Stephanie Todorovich from Perspectives 2. Copyright © 1991 by the Etobichoke Board of Education, Canada. Reprinted by permission.

Watermelons by Charles Simic from *Selected Poems*. Copyright © 1985 by Charles Simic. Reprinted by permission of George Braziller, Inc.

Younde Goes to Town from *The Cow-Tail Switch and Other West African Stories* by Harold Courlander and George Herzog. Copyright 1947 by Harold Courlander. Copyright © 1975 by Harold Courlander. Reprinted by permission of Henry Holt and Company, Inc.

Can We Talk? from 3-2-1 Contact Magazine. Copyright © 1992 by The Children's Television Workshop. Reprinted by permission.

Photo credits

Unit 1

Part Opener
xxii Clockwise from top left: © FourByFive, FPG,
Int'l., © Superstock, FPG, Int'l.
1 Clockwise from bottom left: FPG, Int'l., FPG, Int'l.,
Nino Mascardi/The Image Bank

Text
4 FPG, Int'l.
5 FPG, Int'l.
11 © FourByFive
12 Top to bottom: FPG, Int'l., Bill Gallery/Stock
Boston
26 © Martin Rogers

Unit 2

Part Opener
30 Clockwise from top right: © D. Chawda/Photo
Researchers, Inc., Bill Gallery/Stock Boston

Text
47 Clockwise from top left: © Comstock,
© Comstock, © Stock Imagery, Bob Daemmrich/
Stock Boston, © Marlene Ferguson/Index Stock
Photography, Inc.
53 © Craig Aurnes/West Light
55 Clockwise from top right: Bettmann, © John
Eastcott/Yva Momtiuk/Woodfin Camp & Assoc.,
Inc., © Brian Seed/Tony Stone World Wide, Ltd.,
© D. Chawda/Photo Researchers, Inc., © R. & S.
Michaud/Woodfin Camp & Assoc., Inc., © Robert
Frerck/Tony Stone World Wide, Ltd.
56 Bill Gallery/Stock Boston
57 Ultratec, Inc., Madison, WI
66 Lawrence Migdale/Stock Boston

Unit 3

Part Opener
68 Clockwise from top left: © Comstock,
© Comstock
69 Clockwise from bottom left: © Comstock, FPG
Int'l., © Stock Imagery, © Comstock

Chapter Opener
70 Clockwise from bottom left: © Bob Kramer, Stock
Boston, © Comstock
71 © Comstock

Text
72 Courtesy of John Goddard
73 Clockwise from top right: © Eric Kamp/Index
Stock Int'l., Inc., © Comstock, © Comstock,
© Stock Imagery, © Sullivan/Index Stock Int'l., Inc.,
© Comstock, © Comstock
82 Left to right: © Stewart Cohen/Index Stock Int'l.,
Inc., © Stewart Cohen, © Comstock
83 © Comstock
86 Clockwise from top left: FPG Int'l., © Charles
Feil/Stock Boston, © Phil Cantor/Index Stock
Photography, Inc., AP/World Wide Photos
95 Clockwise from top left: © Comstock,
© Daemmrich/Stock Boston, © Comstock,
© Billy E. Barnes/Tony Stone World Wide, Ltd.
97 © Kenneth Garrett/West Light
98 Clockwise from top left: © Philip Wallick/FPG,
Int'l., © Comstock, © Brooks Kraft/Sygma
99 Clockwise from bottom left: © Comstock, © David
Grossman/Photo Researchers, Inc., FPG, Int'l.
104 © Robert Frerch/Woodfin Camp & Assoc., Inc.

Unit 4

Part Opener
106 © Ullisteltzer
107 Clockwise from top left: Stock Imagery,
© MacDonald Photography/Stock Boston,
AP/World Wide Photos

Chapter Opener
108 Clockwise from top right: © Ullisteltzer,
© Comstock
109 Clockwise from top left: MC Tressin-
Renault/Gamma-Liaison, © Lester Sloan/Woodfin
Camp & Assoc., Inc., © Wolfgang Kaehler

Text
110 © Kindra Clineff/The Picture Cube
116 Clockwise from top left: © Index Stock Int'l.,
Inc., UPI/Bettmann, UPI/Bettmann, © Frank
Pedrick/The Image Works, Bob Hautes/Stock
Imagery, © Comstock
117 Clockwise from top left: Stock Imagery,
© MacDonald Photography/Stock Boston,
© Susan Van Etten
123 © Comstock
131 The Bettmann Archive
132 UPI/Bettmann
133 AP/World Wide Photos
143 Clockwise from top left: © Comstock,
© Comstock, © Comstock, © Comstock

Unit 5

Part Opener
144 Left to right: © Antman/The Image Works, © Index Stock
145 Left to right: © John Lei/Stock Boston, © B. Daemmrich/The Image Works

Chapter Opener
146 Clockwise from bottom left: © Susan Van Etten, © R. Sidney/The Image Works
147 Clockwise from bottom left: © R. Sidney/The Image Works, © Alan Dorow/Actuality Inc., © Index Stock

Text
149 © David W. Johnson
158 © Steve Bourgeois/Unicorn Stock Photos
159 © Susan Van Etten
160 © Antman/The Image Works
165 Left to right: © Stewart Cohen/Index Stock Int'l., Inc., © Stewart Cohen/Index Stock Int'l., Inc.
166 Top to bottom: © B. Daemmrich/The Image Works, © John Lei/Stock Boston
174 © Susan Van Etten
176 Clockwise from top left: © Comstock, © Arnold Jacobs